BEYOND THE LAWS OF

Think

The Science of Being
20 More Secrets

BISHOP E. BERNARD *Jordan*

FOGHORN
PUBLISHERS
"Of Making Many Books There Is No End..."

Beyond the Laws of Thinking
The Science of Being ... 20 More Secrets

ISBN-10: 1-934466-19-0
ISBN-13: 978-1-934466-19-3

Printed in the United States of America

Foghorn Publishers
P.O. Box 8286
Manchester, CT 06040-0286
860-216-5622
www.foghornpublisher.com
foghornpublisher@aol.com

— TABLE OF CONTENTS —

— PROPHETIC PARTNERS —

ᘯ ᘯ ᘯ

I would like to thank each of these prophetic partners for sowing a seed toward this book. Their financial seeds have made it possible for you to be able to receive this book without charge to you. May God add life to every giver, for through your gift you are causing life to perpetuate in others.

Ralph & Gloria Boyce

Debra Campany

Angela M. Carter

Daryl Clark

Mascareen Cohen

Tinika Colclough

Albert Crawford

Regina A. Croswell-Turner

Celena Edwards

Judge Josephine Finn

Tangela Flemming

Sharon Gaines

Dennis Green

Paula Greene

Antoinette Harris

Alice P. Jackson

Teresa Jeter-Newburn

Kimberly Johnson

Bernadine Kelley

Nellie Lane

Marcus Legall

Evelyn Little-Johnson

Bessie Mahone

Michael Perry

Antonia Quinones

Anthony Reid

Cherryl Sharp

Candace Shephard

Brenda Smith

Michelle Starr

Kerney Thomas

Kerney Thomas, Sr.

Sonia Tracey

Eric Walker

Phyllis Whitley

Pastor Lorenzo Williamson

— INTRODUCTION —

◌ ◌ ◌

Why Science and Faith Are NOT Opposites

The book you are holding represents a revolution in human thinking. But it is not because it will tell you anything you didn't already know. No, you have always known this wisdom. What you and most of us living in this material plane lack is clarity. I will give you that clarity and help you understand why the Laws of Being are your golden keys to unlocking limitless prosperity, opportunity and happiness not in the next life, but in this life, the one God created you to live.

When I say "revolution," I also mean "evolution." There is a reason the words rhyme. To evolve is to revolve around a center point of new ideas that challenge what we have been told, challenge how we think in our daily lives. For example, you have been told that science and faith are polar opposites. As a person of spiritual belief, whatever tradition you follow, you have been taught by others to distrust science, to fear it as a tool unbelievers will use to expose faith as a pack of childish lies, a meaningless comfort in the dark. Universities hold symposia where theologians and atheists debate over whether or not science and faith can co-exist, as if they are explosive elements that annihilate each other on contact.

On the other side of the aisle, skeptics and militant atheists like Richard Dawkins and Christopher Hitchens write angry books denouncing faith. Advocates of science wail over the supposed rise of irrationality in our society and the number of Americans who remain "deluded" by religious belief. At the same time, religious fundamentalists campaign against science, insisting that in critical areas like climate change, it cannot be trusted.

All of this is nonsense. Science and faith are not opposed. They are part of the same journey, different tools to seek the same thing: TRUTH. The difference lies only in the nature of the tools. Science is materialistic and naturalistic; nothing can exist outside of nature. It is based on empirical evidence and experimentation. Faith is subjective, based on personal experience that can only be validated by you. If you are a believer, you have probably had at least one deeply spiritual experience that compelled you to commit yourself to God. But if a laboratory asked you to prove that the experience actually happened, could you? Of course not, and it's a ridiculous question. No proof is needed for the subjective. Faith is the substance of things unseen, of the cosmos that lies within each of us.

Science and faith come at truth from different directions. That's all. They dwell in different realms—the worldly and the otherworldly. Therefore they cannot prove or disprove each other, but they can complement one another. Science can use the tools of faith: meditation, intention, self-awareness, what the Buddhists call "lovingkindness." Faith is the haven of the Mind, and the Mind is teaching many things to previously skeptical science. At the same time, faith can and should wield the tools of science: open inquiry, questioning of long-accepted principles, insistence on results. The two disciplines can work together to bring us closer to God's and Man's truth.

The Laws of Being

That is where the first of this extraordinary two-book compendium begins. *The Science of Being* will be followed by *The Science of*

Becoming, and together these two works will illuminate a new landscape of realities about the universe in which we live. Namely, that it is knowable and can be shaped by those who understand the laws that God has placed within it. In my past writings, I have shared some laws with you regarding your thoughts and how to shape your perceptions of who you are, the people in your life, and the way in which Time works to manifest new blessings in your experience. But now we move beyond how you think. Now we're going to look at *who you are.*

In this book, I am going to share with you the 20 Laws of Being. I did not invent these laws any more than a physicist invented the laws of gravity or thermodynamics. I simply came into enlightenment about them. God shared with me His purpose for these Laws, and I now share it with you. The main lesson is this: the Laws are your keys to manipulating the cosmos to yield the things that you want. Like gravity, thermodynamics, the speed of light or inertia, the Laws of Being are absolute; they are always there, always working in the same way, and they are not negotiable. But even though you cannot change them, you can understand them and know how to work within their structure to bring abundance, security, good people, opportunity, health and joy into your earthly existence.

Another way in which the Laws of Being are like the laws of nature is that they're visible. They always have an effect, as long as you know how to see it. For example, the law of gravity is obvious: if you drop a stone, it will always fall to the ground (but hopefully, not on your foot). If you didn't know about gravity, you might never even realize that a law was at work. But it is. In the same way, the Law of Supply and Demand (Chapter 8) is just as visible. When the supply of something drops, its cost always rises. If you know how to look for this, you can see it in action all around you. Scarcity breeds greater demand and greater expense.

What You Will Learn

In this long journey that we're about to take together, you will learn to recognize God's handiwork in the Laws that govern every aspect of day-to-day relations between human beings. God set the Laws of Being in place when He fashioned the material reality in which we reside, but he didn't give us an instruction manual to tell us how they work or even what they are. That would be like giving a student all the answers to a test. We've had to figure the Laws out for ourselves over the centuries, and finally, we have.

In this book, I am going to share with you the essential nature of all 20 Laws of Being—what they are, how they work, how they affect your life, what the consequences are for violating them, and how you can leverage them to benefit your life and to do God's will. In these pages, you will discover:

- The core principles underlying each Law

- God's original intention in setting each Law in place

- The purpose of each Law in governing human society

- How to recognize the Law in action

- The perils of ignoring the Laws

- How to turn the Law to your advantage

In the end, you will gain more than a timeless insight into the Mind of God, the Architect of reality (though that might well be gift enough). You will be gifted with a mental and spiritual arsenal of tools that you can use to shape your world according to the way God intended for it to be. God, at the dawn of time, ordained a future of limitless plenty for you. But that future can only be shaped and made manifest by you, and to do this, you must work within the framework of the Laws. I will teach you how to do precisely that. Then you will see that the keys to the Kingdom do not lie with God. They cannot be found anywhere outside of you. They can only be found within you. You are the heir to God's plans for the universe, and the Laws are your path to that inheritance.

Being and Becoming

It's a grand vision, isn't it? Being heir to the work of the Master? Yet why else do you think He created you and all of humanity? God is pure Spirit, and as such He cannot directly shape events in this, the corporeal plane. So He created Himself as a physical entity, a creature of spirit residing in a material shell, to carry out His will in this, the visible, tangible world of time and age and death and suffering. That is why you are here. You are a spiritual being having a temporary material experience. Think about that! How thrilling to have been charged with the task of carrying out a small part of God's will on earth.

Because you are made in God's image, you are a being of duality as He is. God is simultaneously in Time and beyond Time; this is why He can know all things and shape all outcomes. He is not bound by causality as we are. He exists at the same time in both realms. You are bound by Time (that explains the gray hair and sore knees), but you are also a dual being. In your case, you are simultaneously Being and Becoming. Being means that you exist in the now and are as you have always been. In Being, each moment is its own universe and is filled with possibility.

Becoming is something else again. The universe is never static. Things that do not grow and change eventually decay and die or become obsolete. Change is the natural order of the world, because God is always evolving. Yes, you heard me. God is evolving. He is both eternal and constantly changing, and therefore so are you. Or you should be. Becoming means that you are always moving toward a new destiny, a new vision, a new goal, a new purpose for your life. You are Becoming someone and something new. This is the state God has ordained for you. Being and Becoming at the same time, in the same person. We all share this blessed condition.

What this means is that you must know how to carry out God's vision for your life today, and to understand how to create that vision tomorrow. You must understand the Laws that apply to the work you have before you today and those that will shape the destiny that waits for you sometime in the future of mortal Time. Being and Becoming are your birthright, but they are not guaranteed. There are millions who have no idea of their potential or of the charge God has given them, to shape their corner of the world according to His design. Awareness of Being and Becoming will empower you to become a co-creator with God in turning your part of reality into what you desire for yourself and your fellow man. Ignorance is a thing of the past.

What You Can Expect

In this book, you're going to get a crash course in the Laws of Being. You are going to develop an understanding of what the Laws are and how you can turn them into a new, brighter life as you walk forward along the path that God has designed for you. With knowledge of these Laws in hand, you will find yourself able to:

- Identify patterns in your life that are preventing you from having the things you want.

- Envision your greatest desires and bring them into being.

- Fine-tune your consciousness to see the Laws in action in ways that others cannot.

- Attract good fortune and good people to you by virtue of your use of the Laws to shape events.

- Turn failure into success.

- See your fellow human beings in a new way.

- Discover the Divine in you and break free of negative, self-limiting belief systems.

- Transcend your limitations and live a life of limitless joy and potential.

- Enthrone love and hope as the centerpieces of your existence.

These are extraordinary promises. But the Laws of Being have extraordinary power to change everything. Such a reality is within your reach. Life is both science and an act of faith. Thank you for having faith in my words, and thank you for having the inquiring mind to question what you have been taught and open yourself to these world-changing teachings. In Being, you are Becoming, and in creating your future you are becoming one with God. That is, as Shakespeare said, a consummation devoutly to be wished.

Let's begin our journey.

Master Prophet E. Bernard Jordan

June 2008

1

— THE LAW OF LIFE —

999

"All of creation has come from nothing but it is a very special nothing. It is not a vacuum but contains the potential to become something and create something. White animals are very significant symbols in dreams and myths. Why? Because they represent the blank canvas which can be the foundation for the creation of some remarkable works of art. So out of this so-called nothing comes The One who has created everything. Within that nothing, consciousness, intelligence and energy exist which create the matter and the bodies. We are given bodies for specific reasons. No, they are not provided to malfunction and provide a livelihood for health professionals. They are provided so that we may manifest the work of The One and be Co-developers and evolutionists."

—Bernie Siegel, M.D.
Keynote address to the International Society for the Study
of Subtle Energies and Energy Medicine

In Deuteronomy 30:19, scripture says, "This day I call heaven and earth as witnesses against you that I have set before you life and death, blessings and curses. Now choose life, so that you and your children may live." That is God's primary command to us, His creations, His regents on earth. Live. Live wisely, live boldly, live with love and passion and vision. The Law of Life is that we must all live to our fullest potential. Why? Because we are here to manifest God's will in the material world. That is our purpose—your purpose, my purpose, the purpose of all children from today down through the centuries to come. This is the ultimate law because if you do not obey it, the alternative is death—not just eventual physical death but the death of your possibility and God-granted creative powers. We are the only beings on this planet who bear the creative power of God, the ability to reshape the world according to our visions and beliefs. In Being, we bring the world into being every second. We are shaping the path of the future now, today. You are shaping the path of your future by reading these very words.

...we are here to manifest God's will in the material world.

The essence of life is Choice. God endowed us with free will because even though He knew that we would often make unwise choices, hard experience is the only teacher that humans have ever given attention. There can be no other way. Children must leave home and make their own decisions; the alternative is to be puppets. Choice is our power in this world to shape our destiny, and our choices produce the actions that determine whether we will merely survive or thrive.

In some circles, science is trying to prove that free will is a comforting illusion. Those who adhere to the doctrine of *determinism* hold that all human activity, including the experience of knowing God, is merely chemical and electrical activity in the brain. Since all such activity is supposedly governed by known physical laws, our actions must be governed by those same laws. So we must act certain ways. We have no choice in our actions; a murderer has no choice in killing, by this way of thinking.

This is clearly nonsense. Yes, some of our actions are unconscious, as you know if you have ever talked on your cell phone while driving. You can do many things on "autopilot." But when we build a business, choose to associate with certain kinds of people or meditate to commune with the Lord, we clearly make decisions. We exert our free will. Your life is a tapestry of your choices. Your descendants live because of choices you made. You live because of choices your ancestors made. We create a new generation of creators with each choice.

We exert our free will. Your life is a tapestry of your choices.

ↄ ↄ ↄ

The Responsibility is Yours

This reality can be both thrilling and frightening. On one hand, you are one of the regents of the Almighty. Think about that! You are a being with a spark of the Divine; the Oneness of the universe is alive in you and all around you. You have a sacred purpose. On the other hand, that's a huge responsibility. "God is depending on *me* to enact part of His plan on earth?" you say. Yes. It's a titanic idea. Take comfort from the fact that you are equal to the task if you choose to be. God would not have created you had He not known you could handle the responsibility.

The Law of Life operates in consciousness. Your entire consciousness, the aware part of your mind that connects with Spirit and makes deliberate choices, must be immersed in the law for you to be in obedience to it.

You must conform to the law to fulfill your potential; as Ernest Holmes wrote, "Living without conforming to the law of tragedy."

Affirm All of God's Laws

Not just the Law of Life must be affirmed and assented to by you, but all the Laws of Being. There can be no laws without human recognition that they exist. Again, we come back to science and why it is not in conflict with spirituality as so many insist. For centuries it was assumed that the laws of physics operated independently of any human agency. Gravity pulled objects back to earth, light traveled at 186,000 miles per second, and electricity flowed through power lines. Everyone figured that these laws must be part of the foundation of the universe; it didn't matter whether humans acknowledged them or not, they were in effect.

So the laws of nature are not indifferent to our attentions. In fact, they are dependent upon them.

But now through the area known as quantum mechanics, we have found that the universe is actually dependent on conscious observation! The tiniest particles of matter and energy are actually just probabilities until they are observed by someone, so by observing and acknowledging the existence of matter and energy, we are in a very real way bringing it into existence. So the laws of nature are not indifferent to our attentions. In fact, they are dependent upon them.

So it is with the Laws of Being. Human laws have no power unless we recognize them and agree that they bind us to a code of conduct and morality. With our choices and by making "I am" statements, we give the laws of man's word puissance; we do the same with God's laws. This is theology with *responsibility*. God does not make your decisions for you and hand them down as holy writ; He simply puts the machinery of creation in place and leaves it to you to learn to run it. In this way, no one else can be to blame for your failures, and no one else can take credit for your triumphs. In fact, the greatest disasters in human history have occurred when someone refused to accept responsibility for error. Adam blamed God and Eve for his eating of the apple, resulting in banishment from the Garden of Eden. But God did not make Adam make this decision. Adam made a choice, and one could argue that he deserved banishment from paradise *not* for his defiance of God's edict but for his refusal to take *responsibility* for it. In breaking that essential law of God, Adam sealed his fate.

The Source of Inventive Thinking

The Law of Life stipulates that our purpose is to bring new things into being—ideas, enterprises, children, art, literature, new life forms through fields like genetic engineering and so on. Each human being is at his or her core a creator, and we feel the impulse early on in our lives, when as children we create imaginary worlds in our minds. Oddly enough, this natural inventiveness has its source in sloth, our drive to satisfy our desires with the least work possible. What else has fueled the creation of every invention from the internal combustion engine to the personal computer? It's the desire to do less physical work while being more productive, to spend less time working and more time enjoying. That's why Aladdin had his lamp!

But this same drive also pushes us to be discoverers and explorers. The passion to round the next curve in the road and see what lies out of view may be the defining characteristic of Man. Placed there by God, our need to discover and learn and find answers has led us to conquer new lands, foster incredible science and exercise our own natural creative principle to reshape the world according to our own vision. Rather, we think it's our vision, but it's actually a shared vision with God. All our achievements are the result of the creative fire he placed within us, the product of the invisible mind that works with the physical tool of our brain to create intelligence, intellect and conscious reason. God's creation of Man was the first link in a chain of creation that continues to echo throughout reality.

The Boomerang Effect

"Do unto others as you would have them do unto you." An approximation of what has become known as the Golden Rule is found in Leviticus 19:18 ("...love your neighbor as yourself..."), but it's not a Christian idea. It appears in virtually every culture and every religion. It is a human idea, and it is about much more than simply treating people nicely so they will treat you the same.

The reason this is called the Golden Rule is that the principle of *reciprocity* defines the dynamics by which you can create and receive wealth in this world. You see, the Law of Life says that you must live and create to bring God's plan into existence in your perception, but you cannot do so only for yourself. You must do the same for others as well. You must help others to create and obey this law in order for blessings to manifest in your own life. Put plainly:

ಿ ಿ ಿ

YOU MUST GIVE BEFORE YOU CAN RECEIVE.

ಿ ಿ ಿ

No doubt you have heard this idea expressed countless times in popular culture, but here are the reasons behind it. The "boomerang effect" is a fundamental fact of the cosmos, in that whatever you put out comes back to you. When you are miserly and withhold your blessing, then poverty comes back to you. It may not even be material poverty (there are some terrible people who are very rich) but moral or spiritual poverty, so that the life you buy with your money becomes a curse to you. Money is no guarantee of joy!

When you give to others freely and openly, you activate God's economy, which is based on the flow of energy in all directions. So when you give out, you get back; energy flows back in your direction and breaks blockages that have kept you from receiving material and spiritual wealth. This is why the man who gives to others in the community without any thought of reward or even for his own financial security will inevitably receive not only the gratitude and blessings of others in the community but new opportunity and greater wealth and health coming toward him. The giver obeys the Law of Life by sowing the seeds of new creation, helping others to become creators and live by the law as well.

So when you give out, you get back;

Taking Whose Name in Vain?

I trust that you are beginning to grasp your own power more clearly, although as we proceed through the 20 Laws of Being together the matter will become even clearer. Right now, you should be beginning to understand that your every action and thought has potency in the world, to shape it toward the ends of joy and wealth and health or toward chaos, loss and poverty. You are a co-creator with the Lord; you must govern what you say and do because your thoughts are *things* that have tangible reality outside your brain and affect the world around you.

This lends new meaning to the concept of taking the Lord's name in vain. For centuries, Christians have regarded the idea as a matter of disrespect to God, not much more important than sticking your tongue out at your grandfather (though when I was growing up, that was an offense that would bring the wrath of heaven down on your head and my father's belt down on your behind). But God is not mocked. He is not a petulant child as so many religious texts have portrayed Him. You cannot take the Lord's name in vain. What you can do is take your own name, the "I Am" that is your divine nature, and misuse it, disempowering yourself as a creator.

So you must learn to be wiser and more aware of your words and thoughts as you become a wielder of the Law of Life.

❍ ❍ ❍

In working the Law of Life, it is vital that you exercise great care in your talk about yourself, because your words have the power to shape your future. When you misuse "I Am" by describing yourself as poor, worthless, unhealthy or unloved, you are setting in motion subtle clockwork that may bring those ideas to pass in your physical experience! Taking your "I Am" in vain can poison your good works, and therefore the destiny God has decreed for you. This is the real way that God's name can be taken in vain, by declaring failure and misfortune for yourself. So you must learn to be wiser and more aware of your words and thoughts as you become a wielder of the Law of Life.

More Misconceptions

As you will discover, part of learning the truth about the Science and Laws of Being is unlearning some closely-held misconceptions about God and His relationship to us, His created children. Another of those distorted ideas is that death only comes at the end of physical life and that Hell only exists in the afterlife for those souls who are evil or unrighteous. Both are untrue. In reality, death is a state that can exist for anyone at any time, provided he or she is living outside the Law of Life.

The Law of Life cannot contain death; it is against the Will of God, which is almighty. The only way in which death can come into your life is if you ignore the Law of Life and separate yourself from God. Death is not the end of life; it is being cut off from the Source of your being. When you impose this separation on the Law of Life by rejecting your role as creator and pushing away your responsibility for your thoughts and words, you impose death upon life.

As Dr. Ernest Holmes wrote in *Love and Law,* "This impersonal, eternal law receives the impression of my thought, and if I say, 'Everything is wrong,' it is wrong." When you bring that isolation into your life, you die to God. When you are with God, you are whole. When you are apart from God, you are incomplete. When you are with God, you are connected, networked to all your brethren who are in the same state; when you are without God, you are cut off. When you are with God, you are in Heaven even as you walk the earth. When you are without God, you are in Hell and there is no need for a devil or a lake of fire. Hell is the absence of God. There is so much evil and so much poverty in the world because there are so many impoverished souls who live cut

> *The only way in which death can come into your life is if you ignore the Law of Life and separate yourself from God.*
>
> ᴑ ᴑ ᴑ

off from God and therefore from all others who obey the Law of Life. When you exist in such a state, you can feel it. Loneliness saturates your bones. Now you begin to see what is at stake.

Another common misconception about God is that God is outside of us. That is also a fundamental error in spiritual understanding. Think about it this way. Each of us is a separate physical being from all others, occupying our own position in space. We have our own thoughts, motivations, beliefs and desires. Yet within us resides the DNA given to us by our parents and by their parents before them, and without which we would not have form. But who made that DNA? Who conceived of the idea of a double helix of nucleic acids that would be the blueprint for creating you, a whale or a mosquito? God, of course. God used His creative power to create that which gave you life. God's spiritual DNA is in you, in each of us.

God's spiritual DNA is in you, in each of us.

ᦉ ᦉ ᦉ

So you and God are not separate. When you pray, you are praying, in part, to yourself. You are an individual center of "God consciousness," one small part of the Mind of God made physical and mobile in this material realm. God is pure Spirit; he cannot act directly on the physical. He made you and me to carry out His will, and that deep connection remains. You and God are always of the same mind. You work as a unit. You have *unity*. That is why when you adhere to the Law of Life with all its subtleties, you will experience the sense of unified power and love that comes from God.

The Principles of Life

At the heart of the Law of Life are several vital principles that activate certain portions of the law's power. In order to make full use of the law and bring its full potency to bear in attracting greater wealth and fulfillment into your orbit, you must both grasp and use these principles in your daily life. Let us examine this trio of principles in greater detail.

- **The Forgiveness Principle**—Gandhi said, "The weak can never forgive. Forgiveness is the attribute of the strong." Truer words were never spoken. Forgiveness is a central rite of the Christian faith, as we are forgiven for our sins when we repent and accept Christ. But what about our ability to forgive each other? Our world seems to have become more brutal, cruel and heartless, and I believe that is partially because we have forgotten about the healing power of forgiveness. In a society where we are alienated from one another, it is much easier to nurse grudges and anger than to forgive.

  Yet forgiveness is one sign of a higher consciousness. When you forgive another, even if he or she has wronged you grievously, you proclaim your superior nature. Those who can forgive have no need to hold onto resentment of others to feel empowered; they are complete in themselves and their connection with God. They know that in forgiving, they open the gates to bring themselves forgiveness. Open forgiveness of offense is one of the most healing powers in the universe. You must live by it to be in accordance with the law.

- **The Belief Principle**—God is a patient parent, which means He is willing to sit back and let you make mistakes. This does not make Him cruel or uncaring any more than it makes any human parent cruel or uncaring. It makes Him wise. God will not overrule your gift of free will, that most precious of all possessions. You are free to believe what you will and do what you wish—only be aware that what you believe will always come back to you. If you believe you are a loser, you will be one. If you believe you will never meet a man or woman with whom you can fall in love, then you will not. If you believe you are destined for great things and you will bring your dreams to fruition, you shall.

- **The Meat Principle.** What sustains you? What is the bread and meat for your spirit? Whatever sustains you will reveal your character. If you are sustained by shallow, petty things, by grudges against your fellows men or by hoarding what you have and refusing to give to others, then that will reveal you to be a mean spirit of little vision. Others will see this and reward you accordingly. The results you see from your efforts in life will also reveal your character and your beliefs.

If you've experienced disappointment in some endeavor, it's because you put the wrong appraised value on what you were trying to achieve, or perhaps you elevated something or someone to a position where the thing or person was supposed to bring you hope or fruitfulness. When you value a thing or a person wrongly, you cannot help but be disappointed, because the thing or person is not bound to meet your expectations, only to be what God ordained it to be. If you have been hurt in a relationship or by betrayal in a business, it is because you made the source of your hurt into an idol to be worshiped. You forgot that only you can be the source of your own fulfillment. Your role as God-in-this-world should be your meat and bread at the table.

Can You Think As a God?

"What are humans that you are mindful of them, mere mortals that you care for them? Yet you have made them little less than a god..."

—*Psalms, 8:5-6*

Humans for millennia have wondered why God, who created the heavens and the earth, the stars and galaxies and black holes and supernovae, could care for something as small as Man. The truth is that we are a special creation because as far as we know, we are the only beings in the cosmos who share with God the ability to think and reason—to first envision something that does not yet exist and then by force of will and creative energies, to bring it into existence. That is an extraordinary power.

But it is even more extraordinary for this reason: God only communes with those who think as gods. So when you have made a connection with God's Mind when you were deep in prayer or meditation, you were thinking as a god! Part of having an awakening of the spirit is realizing for the first time that you have within you the ability and the right to commune with God as another Divine being, not just as a humble Man. When you begin making "I Am" statements that define you as a creator with a Divine spark, you gain the ability to communicate with God on His level, as a creator. That comes with responsibility as well: whatever you think about, you must do. Your thoughts gain enormous creative power. So one of the rules of the Law of Life is:

૭ ૭ ૭

GOVERN YOUR THOUGHTS.

૭ ૭ ૭

The Power of Thought

You can see now the incredible might contained in your thoughts. The scope of your thoughts will determine the scope of your achievements. God wants you to think great thoughts and do great things; that is why He rewards those who take great risks, even if in the short run it appears that those risks have produced little. The man who dares will profit and prosper, while the man who thinks small will achieve only small things.

We must work to grow in our thoughts so that as we control our thoughts and their creative potential, we train our minds to think of great tasks, projects, and goals. Why aim to open one neighborhood store when you could open 10? Why try to feed the poor of one city when you could feed the needy of an entire state? The greater your thoughts, the more you will wring out of the fabric of the universe the raw materials to bring those thoughts into existence.

Under the law, what you think is ready to come to pass down the stream of time into the future.

ꩰ ꩰ ꩰ

What happens when we cannot express those great thoughts? We become blocked and frustrated. Our visions back up in our minds and we lose our creative powers. The path to expression is always there, but sometimes we deny ourselves the method of expression. We might insist there simply isn't the money, we don't have the time, or we can't find anyone to help us. That's not acceptable to God's law. Under the law, what you think is ready to come to pass down the stream of time into the future. You must act, even if you see no visible means to make it possible. You must spend that last $100, stay up all night working or start working and letting your spirit attract those who can help you. Not expressing your vision is not an option. It will make you bitter and frustrated.

Breaking the Commandments

Not all laws must be respected in the same way as the Laws of Being. The Ten Commandments are an example. They are not absolute, because they were created by God to govern man's behavior; they are not absolute laws of the universe like the Laws of Being. The Commandments are more like laws against speeding or libel. They have truth at the center, but they are caught up in dogma, which you must avoid.

But God would rather have you creating according to His vision than sitting or kneeling.

၁ ၁ ၁

You may have to break some of the Commandments to live the Law of Life. Does that sound like blasphemy? It may, but it isn't. In reality, what it means is that you must strip away the dogma to find the truth at the heart of these ancient laws. Let's look, for example, at the Commandment that tells us to honor the Sabbath day and keep it holy. Even in the New Testament, God reveals that this order isn't all it's cracked up to be. In Mark 2:27, He says, "...and he said unto them, the Sabbath was made for man, and not man for the Sabbath." In other words, the Sabbath was a concept designed for Man to fit into, but Man was not designed to be slothful on the Sabbath. The people who thought that were the ones who didn't understand God's laws. They thought the way to please God was to sit around all day praying and thinking about him. But God would rather have you creating according to His vision than sitting or kneeling.

It is important to thank God for His blessings and commune with the faith community on Sundays, but it is not necessary to turn the Sabbath into a day when nothing else gets done. Remember, these laws were laid down during the Second Generation of mankind, after the Fall. In the First Generation there were no laws, because we had not separated ourselves from God's thought. When we became idolatrous, laws became necessary. But when you return to that co-equal place where you are one with God's Mind, laws no longer apply.

Everything Must Change and Grow

One of the greatest mistakes some people of faith make is in believing that things will not change. Societal norms must stay the way they were in the 1950s, science must not shed new light on faith and so on. This is impossible. Change is inevitable; even God is evolving toward His future through us, His creations. Human culture changes, knowledge evolves, even churches and religions adapt and grow over time. Nothing that is living can resist change, nor should it. Where there is no change, there is only decay and death. Rather than fear change, you should welcome it with open arms.

The comfort zone is the death zone.

Yes, change can be frightening, but imagine if you never went through that discomfort or risk or time of feeling like you were falling from a great height without a parachute? You would still be in kindergarten enjoying your milk and cookie break, afraid to step out into the wider world away from the teachers who make you feel comfortable. The comfort zone is the death zone. We cannot live there for long, or we end up merely existing. The Law of Life demands that we exit and seek change in all its forms.

When you know this and embrace this great truth, the Law of Life will come to meet you in your daily routine. You will see how your thoughts manifest in all things. The mind of God resurrects itself in you, and in each of us who live the Law of Life. Mental action shapes the universe; it is how God first brought the universe into being. When your mental attitude is one of knowing your "I Am" and declaring what will be by your word, you bring God's Word into play. You must live with confidence and knowledge balanced with humility and kindness.

Grow or Go

As you can see even in this first chapter, the Laws of Being are for grownups. A thrilling but terrifying responsibility rests on your shoulders whether you are 18 or 80, a regular churchgoer or one who rarely praises God. You bear a share of the weight for creating the world as it will be tomorrow, next year and next century. There is no theological babysitting available; you need to either walk with God or leave His side so as not to let your negative thoughts bring down the works of others. If you can' grow, you've got to go.

Wealth comes in many forms.

Ralph Waldo Emerson said, "To think is to act." But he also asserted that a man can never rest on past successes. God demands that you always be moving forward—Becoming as well as Being. God created the world in the deeps in six days and then rested, but after his siesta He was right back at it, working hard guiding Man and helping human thought along in its journey to consciousness. The tasks you take on as part of your responsibility to the Law of Life do not need to be earth-shaking; not everyone was meant to start a company, have a music career or cure AIDS in Africa. But you can focus your energies on wellness for yourself and others, on kindness and mercy, and on healing and prosperity for the impoverished. Wealth comes in many forms.

In the end, YOU are the Law of Life. To fulfill it you need to live your life with no visible means of support other than your Divine nature and trust in God. You have everything you need to fulfill your desires while you are on the material plane. God wants you to fulfill them. That is why He made you. It's your choice.

2

— THE LAW OF CAUSE AND EFFECT —

ↄ ↄ ↄ

Life is a perpetual instruction in cause and effect.

—*Ralph Waldo Emerson*

In Luke 6:38, Scripture says, "Give, and it will be given to you. Good measure, pressed down, shaken together, running over, will be put into your lap. For with the measure you use it will be measured back to you." That is a biblical description of one of the basic laws of the universe: the Law of Cause and Effect. If you have any acquaintance with science, you'll know this law spoken of like this: for each action there is an equal and opposite reaction. Well, the physical laws of causality are mirrored in our spiritual realm and with even more power and consequence. You cannot hope to prosper unless you understand the effects that your choices yield.

Understand that in the scientific world, causality—the idea that cause always precedes effect—has been taking a beating in recent years. Physics experiments have shown that nothing in modern quantum mechanics prevents effects from preceding causes, or causes moving backward in time. This may mess with our common sense, but those of us versed in God's economy and the actions of Spirit know that cause and effect are never as simple as throwing a ball and watching it bounce. Actions have repercussions that vibrate throughout reality. Thoughts possess the same power. When you give, you set in motion your own opportunity to receive. When you refuse and deny, you make your own denial in future time inevitable.

God Does Not Punish

One of the most common misconceptions about God is that He punishes his children for their mistakes. This is untrue. Instead, punishment for our misdeeds comes from us in the form of the consequences of our choices, thoughts and actions. Hell is a state of being that we create for ourselves in this life by our choices.

> *We each earn our reward or punishment with what we say and do and how we obey God's Laws of Being.*
>
> ○ ○ ○

We each earn our reward or punishment with what we say and do and how we obey God's Laws of Being. When we follow the Law of Life, when we act towards our fellows with kindness and justice, when we live with vision and courage, we reap tremendous rewards that are not always material. Respect, love, community, health—these are all just as valuable as money. And that is vital, because there are people who treat their fellow humans with hate, cynicism and corruption, yet are financially prosperous. But love, peace, respect and community? They will never enjoy these rewards. And as God's children, we need those forces in our lives. Without them, the spirit corrodes.

We are the authors of our own misery. Be wary of this as you begin your journey. As I have said, govern your thoughts until they are laser-focused on what you want and what is good and great.

The Power of Attention

Back to science for a moment. At this exciting time, when the material and non-material are finally converging in a scientific world that is largely free of religious and anti-religious dogma, experiments are showing that the focused intention of the human mind can truly affect the material world. Work in a field known as Distant Mental Influence on Living Systems, or DMILS, is showing without doubt that focused attention can affect the growth of plants, the formation of water crystals, and the cells of the heart. Our minds are connected to all things and our thoughts can heal, grow or kill.

This power goes far beyond the world of molecules and individual cells to our entire existence. Whatever you attend to becomes your experience. When you turn your attention to something, you bring it closer to coming into being. If it already exists, you bring it into your orbit. For example, when you think about the kind of small business you would like to start from scratch, you bring it closer to your material perception. You set forces in motion that bring that business nearer to reality. The more specifically you think about it, the more specific a shape it takes. When you are highly specific in your thinking (this is one of the benefits of business plans—to focus your

> *When you turn your attention to something, you bring it closer to coming into being.*
>
> ☺ ☺ ☺

mind), you will attract astonishingly specific effects into your sphere. The seemingly random but significant effects that psychologist Carl Jung called synchronicities begin this way.

If you focus on something that already exists—a small business that's already operating but that you would love to purchase, for instance—then you will bring it closer to you. The owner of the business might turn out to be a neighbor or a member of your church, or you might suddenly inherit some money that could go towards purchasing the business. That is the power of attention.

Another aspect of this power is that it is immutable. That means there is never a time when our focused intention is NOT manifesting in the world somewhere. At all times, our thoughts are broadcasting from our brains into the interconnected reality of which we are a part and shaping tiny events in that reality, setting small balls rolling. Well, as you know, tiny events can magnify into huge life changes for better or worse. Your thoughts are continually reaching into your surrounding reality and shaping it in your image. That is why people who are habitually pessimistic tend to get negative results in their lives. They create them. This is a law of the cosmos over which we have no control. You cannot change God's law, so you must control your mind.

You cannot change God's law, so you must control your mind.

♡ ♡ ♡

Thinking is Action

In *Creative Mind,* Ernest Holmes writes, "Man is surrounded by a great universal thought power which returns to him always just as he thinks. So plastic, so receptive is this mind, that it takes the slightest impression and molds it into conditions... We must not only think but we must know. We have to provide within ourselves a mental and spiritual likeness for the thing desired... Whatever is imaged is brought forth from mind into manifestation."

That is the perfect explanation for the power of the Mind. Your thoughts are the cause of your good or bad fortune, because your thoughts define what you can do. They determine what can or cannot come into your life. For example, if you focus only on making just enough money to pay your bills, you will never have extra money. If you want abundance, you must focus on abundance. Even more powerful:

○ ○ ○

YOU MUST ACT AS THOUGH THE ABUNDANCE ALREADY EXISTS.

○ ○ ○

As Ralph Emerson Tyne stated, you build whatever is in you. There is nothing you can create in this world that does not already exist within you as thought. If you cannot envision it, then you cannot create it or bring it to pass. If you cannot hold that vision in your mind, then God has ordained that that something is not your destiny. That is why some people were "meant" to be doctors while others were "meant" to be musicians. The doctor can "see" himself working with patients in his mind, while the musician can "see" the notes and chords of a musical composition.

If you can think it, you can become it. In fact, if you think it you will become it without exception. When you run a business, if you want to make more money, turn away lower-paying customers. Turn away business and focus only on attracting higher-paying customers. As soon as you adopt a higher-paying *mindset*, those customers will come.

Natural Law = Spiritual Law

We have created a false dichotomy when it comes to natural versus spiritual law. We talk about faith and science and pit them against one another as if they can never do anything but scorn each other. But the people who do that usually do so for political reasons, not because spiritual and natural laws are really so much in opposition. Truth be told, they are very much of a piece. All natural law is spiritual law. The laws of nature obey the same principle of focused attention that the world of men and God obeys. Otherwise, why would cells heal and water crystals become more beautiful when they are treated with loving intention? Our minds have the power to shape the laws of physics and chemistry. Nature and Spirit are one. That presents us with a vast field of potential creation.

All natural law is spiritual law.

ꙩ ꙩ ꙩ

But as Dr. Holmes stated, you must understand the law before you can apply it properly. In his book *Change Your Thinking, Change Your Life,* he pointed out how race consciousness and the psychology of a group can affect our patterns of thinking and set in motion events of which we can have no conception. We cannot even see the results of thinking that, for instance, demonizes a certain race or sows terror and paranoia in a population until it is too late. The effects of such poisonous mental attention are too subtle to perceive, but I will tell you something: the mindset of the Cold War led directly to the September 11 tragedy. When we plant thoughts of paranoia and intolerance in the psychic ecosystem of Man as we would plant seeds in a field, we should not be surprised with hate, fear and violence are the crop we reap.

You will live according to the long-term level at which your mental state settles. A single day of positive thinking that brings God's economy into play is no match for 20 years of habitual limited thinking. The level of your thought determines the level of your life. If you become OK with just making enough money to be comfortable, that is all you will make. The universe will deflect opportunity and ideas from your awareness that could make you more money, because after all, you have set the rules. Your thoughts have *told* the cosmos the way things are. This is why, if you wish to lead a different life, you must begin training your thinking NOW.

> *The level of your thought determines the level of your life.*
> ❾ ❾ ❾

You Are the Lawmaker

We talk a great deal about God in our writings and our meditations on the universe, and for good reason: God is the Architect of all this natural and spiritual clockwork by which reality operates at all levels. But this can give the false impression that we are under God's control, that He has some ability to reach into our lives and overrule our decisions and judge us. Nothing could be further from the truth. God is pure Spirit; He cannot act on our material plane directly. He can merely advise, counsel and communicate, like a parent speaking with a child who is away at college and can only share wisdom. Now, God's ability to inspire, guide and inform is immense and wields incredible power, but in the end, as with a human parent, He must leave us free to make our own decisions. This can be frightening, because it means God is not around to bail us out when we make mistakes. Once in a while He might inspire someone else to act as His proxy and bring us redemption. But usually, we are on our own.

However, in His great wisdom, God has shared with us the secrets of his Laws and told us how we can prosper and live according to the laws underpinning the universe. That means that, rather than be frightened, we should rejoice. We are free to live as we wish! Each of us is infinite in our universe, with the power to decide our health, wealth and happiness. Each of us is a cosmos in our minds, and that is glorious.

We are free to live as we wish!

ᕣ ᕤ ᕣ

This means that you are the only one who can break the Laws of Being for yourself, as Joel Smith stated. You are the lawgiver in your personal cosmos; all the power lies in your choice, in the habits of thinking that you adopt for yourself. You do not need to ask God for anything other than the continued inspiration and wisdom to make right choices. By following the Laws and achieving your true potential, you honor Him. This also means something that is so momentous and earth-shaking that you may choose not to believe it, but it is quite true:

ᕣ ᕤ ᕣ

GOD HAS NOTHING TO DO WITH GOOD OR EVIL.

ᕣ ᕤ ᕣ

It's true. God created everything in a neutral state. Humans determine good or evil based on the choices we make. Good and evil—Go(o)d and (D)evil if you choose to look at them that way— are in us all, and our choices set the effects in motion that decide what happens to others. We then interpret those events as good or evil. Remember, what is good for one can be evil for another.

Bombing a cave in Afghanistan where Taliban fighters are hiding might be good for the families who lost loved ones on 9/11, but that same choice might be evil for the mothers of young Taliban men who are killed in the bombing.

Much as conservative people are not fond of acknowledging the idea that good and evil are relative concepts, that is the truth. There are few absolutes; there are only choices. The only lasting absolute in human life on this material plane is that your every thought is an action aborning, and that action, whether it is of your hand or the hand of someone who was motivated by your thought, will affect your life for good or evil.

...action, whether it is of your hand or the hand of someone who was motivated by your thought, will affect your life for good or evil.

☾ ☾ ☾

The Cause is All In Your Head

So the essence of the Law of Cause and Effect is that the cause is all in your mind. Thoughts and the words they provoke set into motion invisible machinery in the material world that bring into being the effect—the tangible thing that comes into your awareness. As John Randolph Price stated, thought is form. Thoughts are things that vibrate on a level that cannot be seen or perceived by our ordinary five senses, but exist very much in reality.

According to purely materialist scientists, thoughts are nothing more than the accidental consequences of chemical and electrical brain activity. But this reductive philosophy ignores reality. How many times have you thrown a thought or desire into the wider world like a stone cast into a pond only to have the ripples it created come back to you in the form of what you desired, perhaps days, weeks or months later? How many times have you needed a specific amount of money for something only to have a new job or a raise in pay come along providing exactly that amount of extra money? Do you really think this can be coincidence?

It isn't. Your thoughts wield causative power in the real world. In fact, your thoughts *are* the real world; material experience is but a shadow of the mental reality that emanates from all of us. Each man and woman is a producer of mental reality, a co-creator with God. The real universe is one of energy, and that energy takes the shape of money. Let me state that again:

ɔ ɔ ɔ

MONEY IS ENERGY.

ɔ ɔ ɔ

And all this time you thought that money was something you got paid by someone else for work performed! If you think in such a limited frame about money, then your supply will be limited all your life. Think about money as what it is: the energy to bring about change. Money moves people and changes thoughts, and so it is the power source for changing reality. When money comes into your hands, it creates the awareness of possibility and creation. This changes the thinking of other people, which eventually brings about changes in the material world—new businesses, homes, organizations that aid the needy and so on. But you cannot proceed from the position of needing money in order to change your thinking, or you will always live in want. You must feel the money in your consciousness before you have it in your hands, and it will come to your hands.

In truth, real money is your *thinking* of money as already existing—of already holding the power of change in your hands. When you live every day and moment in that state of mind, material money will respond to your awareness of yourself as the agent of change, and that money will materialize as the Benjamins you are so fond of. What we expect in our minds is what we get in our material world! If you recognize that money is energy, you can radiate that energy from your being at all times and bring that monetary energy to you as surely as a flame attracts moths.

Money moves people and changes thoughts, and so it is the power source for changing reality.

☾ ☾ ☾

Younger and Healthier

As the Law of Cause and Effect goes for money, so it goes for health as well. You will bring ill or good health to yourself by virtue of how and what you think. Now, in the wake of the popular book *The Secret,* critics have sneered at that book's principles by saying it suggests that someone who gets cancer must have willed themselves to develop the disease. This is obviously absurd. No one in his right mind walks around for ten years saying, "I really wish I would develop colon cancer." However, when you violate the Law of Cause and Effect and think negative thoughts about your health, you can set off a subtle cascade effect that eventually leads to diseases like cancer.

Remember, your thoughts not only drive your actions, but they attract certain things into your orbit depending on whether your attitude is empowered and optimistic or defeatist and pessimistic. This brings up the nature of sin. The word "sin" in the Bible is translated from the Greek *hamartia*, which means "to miss the mark." That is, to sin is to fail to achieve an ideal. In the context of God's system of Laws, to sin is to fail to live according to the Laws. So sickness or chronic poor health is a direct result of failing to observe the laws that would bring you good health—failing to govern your mind in a way that brings vitality to your body and instead thinking thoughts that attract disease. Look at the word: *dis-ease.* When your mind is ill at ease, you bring illness into your body!

That also means that the secrets to staying younger and living longer and healthier are within your mind. Simply don't sin. Train your mind. Here are three simple rules for staying younger:

1. Never respond to stupidity in others. You can't talk someone out of anything. Most of us respond only to hard experience, rarely to the wisdom of others. Wasting your time in contact with another's foolishness can only pollute your lawful thinking.

2. Eat when you're hungry. Sleep when you're tired. Keep it simple.

3. Eat bananas. They're a perfect, complete food that fuels mind and body. More important, eat whole, simple foods unaltered by man.

Youthful living for all your 80, 90 or 100 years is not a matter of the body. There are many slender, fit people who die at 60 and many overweight people who live into their 90s because they have a hopeful, purposeful, forward-looking mentality. They know better than to bring negative health consequences into their awareness by thinking them into existence. They live with purpose and an eye on the future, no matter how old they are. That, my friends, is wisdom.

Mastering the World

If it is not clear by now, let me state it simply: you are the master of your existence. God has given you the freedom to choose and the power to make your choices manifest in reality. You have only to choose rightly. As Vernon Howard wrote in *Inspire Yourself:*

A citizen said to a famous reformer, "Please explain. You condemn society for violence, yet your protests are equally violent."

"There is a big difference," said the reformer.

"You demand that other people respect you, but you never speak of your need to respect them."

"There's a big difference."

"You criticize other groups for putting on pressure, yet the entire purpose of your group is to apply pressure."

"There is a big difference."

"What is the big difference?"

"How stupid you are. We are good, while others are evil."

A man can be empowered by delusion or by self- knowledge, but only self-insight changes anything.

It is your purpose to master your reality through your consciousness. When you gain self-insight, you transcend the limitations most of us put on ourselves. Most people see themselves as powerless, pushed to and fro by forces beyond their control. But you have in your hands the information that can free you from that impotent delusion. Mastery is your birthright and your responsibility. You are charged with taking control of your corner of the material universe and reshaping it according to God's Laws, and in the process making it better, more just, more productive and more prosperous for others as well.

Keep in mind that others will not understand this mode of thinking. They are still in thrall to the idea of God as overlord making all the decisions. They are not ready for this ultimate responsibility, and so they cannot be relied upon to transform their personal experience or their corner of the physical realm. That is why leaders exist. Some people are ready to wield the Laws of Being, others need teaching, and some will never be ready. You must take up the burden for those who cannot obey the laws; you must become a master.

> *...you must become a master.*
>
> ☉ ☉ ☉

Out-Picturing

Emmet Fox called "scientific prayer" the golden key to health, wealth and happiness. Prayer invokes the Law of Cause and Effect by doing what is called "out-picturing": taking a mental image of the specific effect you desire and projecting it into the spiritual realm, where God's laws can work on it. That is what I call the *active* use of God's laws, when you choose your thought and choose the result you want. When you choose your thoughts, you choose your future experience.

Passive use of the laws is when you maintain an "I Am" state of mind at all times, a visionary, positive, prosperous state of mind that acts as if what you want to achieve is already achieved. Both will bring about results, but prayer for a precise result will bring about results faster.

These two modes of mental discipline will enable you to become what you were created to be: a mirror image reflecting the glory of God, the Architect and Scientist behind the structure of the universe. That mirror reflects who you can be and become; when you look in it, you are seeing the Divine nature of yourself. But if you are not living up to that nature—if you are not following the Law of Cause and Effect and disciplining your mind, don't blame the mirror. God is not to blame. The mirror doesn't need fixing.

If you want to change things, fix yourself. Just as you are a mirror image of God, the world you experience every day is a reflection of your mind. Your thoughts and beliefs become the actions and events that make up the tapestry of your days. If you change who you are and how you think, you will change your experience. Believing is action. Change begins with belief, then gets translated to action. Belief is cause, action the effect, and change the result. Out-picture the state of your world as being different than it is today, pray for the specific effects that will bring about that new world, and then act and think as if they are already realized. You will see the transformation of your experience, and it is miraculous.

If you want to change things, fix yourself.

〇 〇 〇

Life and the Law

Due to the Law of Cause and Effect, when you beat up life, the Law of Cause and Effect will beat you up in return. The Law of Life, remember, is the heart of everything. You must live according to the idea that life is the force that sets God's vision in motion and achieves what He intends. So when you punch life in the stomach by ignoring that truth, cause and effect will inevitably land a few punches in return. You might find yourself in economic ruin, with poor health, or losing important relationships.

There is no escape from this causality. It is an essential rule of existence. All the Laws of Being work together, each reinforcing the other in the intricate, complex web of God's handiwork. Live life according to the laws, and you will find wonderful effects moving toward you, reminding you of the astonishing, blessed power of your Mind.

3

— THE LAW OF HARMONY —

꩜ ꩜ ꩜

Happiness is when what you think, what you say, and what you do are in harmony.

—Mahatma Gandhi

Harmony occurs when you recognize that you and the Power that shapes the universe are One. Nothing happens independently of attention; quantum mechanics has established that an observer is required to create reality out of probability. So when the Bible in John 10:30 says, "I and my Father are one," the passage is truly stating that you and God are the same being clothed in different forms—you in flesh, God in Spirit. This recognition of truth has incredible power, as Ernest Holmes wrote in *365 Science of Mind:*

"My recognition of the Power is sufficient to neutralize every false experience, make the crooked straight, and the rough places smooth. Definitely I know that this recognition establishes the Law of Harmony in my experience, the Law of Prosperity, the sense of happiness and health. I experience complete Wholeness."

Harmony is essential to working the Laws of Being. It is not enough to know the rules and understand the workings of God's laws; you must know that you are at one with them and with God, sharing His power to shape reality. You must have that revelation. This is not an easy thing to do in a faith landscape where are constantly told that God is judging us, that God disapproves, or that God is always looking for a reason to cast us into the fires of Hell. Asserting your Divine Oneness can seem like heresy, but the greatest leaps in faith are often cloaked in heresy.

If you have this revelation, you will see the truth and gain the power to control your destiny. If you remain ignorant to the truth, your life will forever be one of chance, luck and circumstance. You will be subject to the changing winds of fortune and have no sense of a greater purpose. You will be at odds with the will of God, and therefore in a kind of Hell on earth. Only when you open your mind to the truth and step away from fear and superstition can you have the revelation of harmony.

Heaven is in Your Mind

Consciousness is everything. Many scientists who research the complex problem of consciousness now believe that it is a fundamental building block of reality, perhaps even predating things like electrons and even light itself. That is no surprise to we who walk with God's Laws. We know that before there was anything, there was God, the Cosmic Consciousness, the Chief Scientist of existence. We are mirror images of that Consciousness, sharing in its causative power to create and affect this world.

Consciousness is elemental and irreducible. As such, when you hold a truth in your consciousness, you will experience that truth. You will bring that truth to you as a magnet attracts iron. Let me make this even plainer:

ღ ღ ღ

YOU ARE YOUR THOUGHTS.

ღ ღ ღ

You are not your limited physical body, prone to disease and injury and age and death. Your body is merely a shell created for your consciousness so that you can act on the material plane and work God's Will. Your body will decay when you die, but your consciousness—your Spirit—will continue, because it is part of God's Consciousness and therefore immortal. So don't be fooled by appearances: your thoughts are your identity and your reality. What you think will come to pass; you've seen in this in your life many times. Think empowered, productive thoughts and good things come your way, but expect the worst and that is what becomes real in your experience. When you see the truth of the power of your mind, you obey the Law of Harmony. You begin to free yourself from all limitations on wealth, health, and happiness.

It is your mind that enables you to reach the sublime state where all is possible and you live without limits.

ღ ღ ღ

Taking that to its logical conclusion, we may say that Heaven is not a place in the clouds, but is in the mind of each one of God's children. God's Kingdom is not a location, but a set of Laws. It is your mind that enables you to reach the sublime state where all is possible and you live without limits. As Emmet Fox stated, the Law of Harmony demands that you believe in your own divinity and perfection before you can enter Heaven. Believing that you have limitations or are less than Divine is a false belief, that the Law states that no one with a false belief can enter into Heaven. Blasphemy is not disbelief in God; it is disbelief in the mastery of your own mind over all things in your reality: your health, your prosperity, your relationships and your freedom. You MUST believe and know these things to be true in order to have the perfect health and wealth that God has ordained for you. To do anything less is a denial of God.

The Movement of Mind

We're going deep in this chapter, and I hope you're with me. The things I'm saying can sound intimidating, but what I'm really asking you to do is re-educate your mind to hold the truth of your role as co-creator with God as self-evident as the fact that the sun will rise or rain will fall. You don't question these things; they Are. Your existence as a proxy for God, with a Mind that moves toward perfection, is also something you must perceive as simply Being, without question.

This is Harmony: When you can redefine your Self as a Mind walking around in a body, a Mind connected to the wholeness of God and all the other fully realized Minds in the world, understanding and accepting that this Harmony is omnipotent. When you know this and breathe it without thinking, you are in Harmony with God.

Nothing moves but Mind, as Dr. Holmes has said. That is what you must internalize above all else. When you want to bring about change in your world, do not act with your hands. Move your mind and the actions will follow. Meditate and pray on what you want to achieve and you will set forces in motion.

Healing the Discord

One of the most profound effects of being in accordance with the Law of Harmony is that it heals and brings peace. When you live in knowing that you are One with God and all His enlightened creatures, doubt and fear are banished. Paradise truly becomes attainable in this life. Harmony removes the discord in your mind. As we can often do, we look at the word for hints as to its true meaning. Discord equals *dis-chord,* a dissonance of music or lack of harmony. So when you are not living in accordance with the Law of Harmony—when you do not act and think and breathe as one who is One with the Divine—you experience discord. This can take the form of stress, fear, doubt, frustration, lack of money, marital argument, misfortune or even illness.

...inner harmony spreads outward and heals the discordance of others around you.

When you come into harmony, you make that dissonant music beautiful again. Coming into a harmonic state with the Laws of Being creates peace in your mind and Spirit. What is even more astonishing is that this inner peace leads to outer peace, not only for you but for others. Just as music cannot be confined to one location but must spread outward in waves to other listeners, inner harmony spreads outward and heals the discordance of others around you. You become a channel of peace for multitudes, resonating through your community, your city or even your world. As Joel Goldsmith wrote in *Consciousness Transformed,* "When you have an inner experience, you have opened out a way for the imprisoned splendor to escape, and this becomes a Law of Harmony to you, your mind, your body, your home, your business and to any receptive member of your family."

In this way, your own inner harmony creates the healing life and the physical and mental health that you desire. Instead of abdicating responsibility for your health to doctors and drugs, you should take control of it by accepting that your mental state creates your physical state. When you are in harmony in your Spirit, you will have vitality of the body. Illness and disability are reflections of a mind and Spirit awash in conflicted music, denial and ego. That is why you must always confront defeatist and disempowering thoughts. What you do not confront, you cannot change. Train your mind to exist in a state of harmony.

Truth Replaces Error

Simply put, harmony is the result of seeing the truth about existence, God and Man—of letting go of erroneous and outdated roles and ideas. The ancient, oppressive idea that we are "sinners in the hands of an angry God," which was clearly a device designed to manipulate and control an ignorant populace, is replaced with a holistic vision of Man as sharing the Divine essence with God. We are God's proxies, not his subjects. When you can see and live that truth and govern your mind according to the Laws, harmony is inevitable. Your consciousness is instantly and forever transformed to a higher resonance.

We are God's proxies, not his subjects.

♡ ♡ ♡

When truth drives out error, you have declared yourself to be a higher being with an enlightened perception. That really is all it takes: to declare your "I Am" in God-consciousness. The mistake many people make is by going on and on about God-this and God-that and praising and singing hosannas. That might be what a church expects, but it's not what God wants. Remember, God wants only one thing from you:

ᥴ ᥴ ᥴ

FOR YOU TO BECOME A CREATOR BY LIVING THE LAWS OF BEING.

ᥴ ᥴ ᥴ

We spend so much time focusing on God being great—buttering up God, really. We do it because we're afraid not to, just like the many people who go to church not because they want to but because they are afraid not to. Well, what if I told you that you could stop going to church today and for the rest of your life and God would not care? I'm not saying you should do this, because church fills many important roles. It connects you to others in the faith community, gives you a way to financially support important works, and reminds you of vital lessons. But those are things that matter to man, not God. If you want to please God, you have nothing more to do than to live every second of your life by His laws, and benefit from their power.

Your focus should be on yourself, on the God in you, rather than on God the Father. When you declare your perfect life and perfect yourself according to these laws, you complete God's creative act.

Harmony Comes From the Mind of God

So it is possible to achieve harmony with the universe by perfecting your own mind, but where did harmony itself come from? Just as with music, you can play or sing the notes, but you did not create the idea that is music. In the case of cosmic harmony and earthly music, the credit belongs to God. Harmony exists only in the mind of God, and humans whose minds are functioning at a Divine level, with pure awareness of their creator nature and a declaration of their "I Am," tap into that infinite source of harmony.

Often this harmony will take the form of money flowing from an unknown source into your conscious experience. Remember that money is the physical manifestation of the energy needed to create change; when you are truly in harmonic consciousness, you will never need to worry about money. The activity of truth taking place in our consciousness blesses not only us but all around us, writes Joel Goldsmith, bringing harmony to those we are thinking about consciously but also to those who are in our minds unconsciously.

When you open your Self to that Source of limitless harmony, you destroy the idea of limits.

ᘐ ᘐ ᘐ

When you open your self to that Source of limitless harmony, you destroy the idea of limits. Limitations are the only sin you can commit, because when you place artificial limits on yourself, you deny your godly nature. You deny God one of his proxies on this material plane. That is sinful. Instead, you are called to *know* that you are without limitation and can bring into being any vision that you can hold in your mind. Those entrepreneurs, activists and athletes who achieve seemingly superhuman results? There's nothing about them that is different from you—EXCEPT their refusal to think about limitations. Their entire focus is on the will to achieve and the knowledge that they bear the power within them to create what they wish.

Centered In Truth

At some point, the discussion must come back to the rewards to be enjoyed by people who follow the Laws of Being. We all want to make more money, to live in a fine home, to be healthy and respected and wise and loved. So I'm often asked, "Do I have to do anything more than know the Laws to reap the rewards?"

Yes, you do. Harmony only rewards those people who are centered in truth, the truth that your consciousness is the Divine nature of existence. You cannot simply know this truth to realize your true potential; you must *become* this truth. This is why many people become confused about why their positive thinking and can-do attitudes don't get the kinds of blessed results that others enjoy. I tell them it's because blessings are not about what you do or what you think; you can think like you are obeying the Law of Harmony but it can be nothing more than window dressing. You must be the law of harmony. Your consciousness must be built on that truth for your thoughts to take form and bring those rewards into your physical awareness.

It is not what we do but who we are that sets the wheels of great change in motion. If we are agents of truth, then the power to set those wheels in motion radiates from within us without our volition. As Goldsmith says, we ourselves can do nothing. In our physical abilities, we remain limited mortals. But within our consciousnesses, we wield the power to move worlds. We can do nothing alone. Truth must illuminate our path while our innate Divine selves reach beyond space and time to create, inspire or accumulate. There is nothing you can do to make such miracles occur. They either happen because you have chosen to be a person centered in the Truth of the Laws, or they do not happen at all. Consciousness is reality.

Consciousness is reality.

ᝐ ᝐ ᝐ

Spiraling Upward

As you digest this, understand that there is nothing to fear. You are on a glorious journey to discover and develop what John Randolph Price calls your Master Self. For centuries, few humans knew this. This information was not available, and science as we know it did not exist. Only a few splendidly enlightened individuals grasped it intuitively in a place beyond the thinking mind: Martin Luther King, Jr., Gandhi, Thomas Jefferson, Harriet Tubman. People of extraordinary vision and creative power, who could move mountains. They understood. But you are present at a time when this understanding is accessible to anyone who wishes to see. That is thrilling!

It is the consciousness that is a reflection of God and does His work.

You are constantly on a journey from your lower self to your Master Self. Each step you take toward living the Truth of the Law of Harmony, you make another leap toward your Master Self. What is your Master Self? It is that state of consciousness that is free or doubt and fear and always operates in the mode of positive, visionary thought that brings good into existence. It is the consciousness that is a reflection of God and does His work. You are always spiraling upward from a simpler, sleeping self to a higher, nobler state. You are becoming part of the Divine Order.

The Practice of Harmony

Harmony becomes more than a Law. It becomes a practice that elevates not only your own consciousness but those of the people in your sphere.

Like a martial art, the practice of harmony gradually transforms your being, turning deliberate thought patterns into habitual ones until your practice of harmony becomes who and what you are. At some point, the martial artist ceases thinking about his discipline, attitude and defensive moves and becomes them; they are his very nature. The same occurs with the Law of Harmony. As you practice training your mind and immersing your consciousness in the Divine oneness of God's Laws, you will evolve beyond practice to being.

The practice of harmony delivers rewards to any person in accordance with his or her willingness and commitment to achieve perfect harmony. Basically, you get out of living what you think you will get out of it. The more you are out of harmony, the more you will find yourself with limitations on what you can achieve. This is a danger to all of us who are enlightened, because the great mass of humanity does not share out insight and spiritual development. Human society is a jungle that drives everything and everyone to mediocrity. Notice that great, world-changing ideas are almost always regarded at first with anger or scorn. The unenlightened jungle wants you to be consumed. Know this:

の の の

ANYTHING THAT IS AVERAGE IN YOUR LIFE IS AN
ENEMY TO YOU LIVING TO YOUR FULL POTENTIAL.

の の の

When you reach the point where harmony is not only a practice but the center of your being, when you are living every second in full participation as an aware co-creator with God and declaring your "I Am" to bring blessings into your life, averageness is an enemy. You must reject average people, average ideas and average results. They will only bring you down. Living by the Laws means becoming an *aspirational* being.

Think in Alignment With Spirit

What you believe, you will achieve. Great words, right? But is it really than simple? Yes, because it's not your mind that does the believing. It's your Spirit. Remember, we are creatures of physicality and Spirit, our bodies created to house our Spirits. God is pure Spirit, and our Spirits are tethered to God throughout our physical lives on earth. So where our bodies are ignorant, our Spirits know. Your Spirit has already seen what you can and will accomplish in this life! Your Spirit knows what you can do long before your mind does—in fact, your Spirit has *always* known what you are capable of. When you are fully in harmony, you are in alignment with your Spirit, and that is when you will become rich, whole, loved and successful.

> *If you send desperation and need out into the universe, you will receive the same in return.*
>
> ☾ ☾ ☾

You buy what you have in your life with your belief in yourself, not with your money. Self-belief in your ability to manifest what you want in your awareness is the currency of God's economy. Of course, this is a double-edged sword, because you can also throw that buying power away as surely as tossing your wallet into the trash. This is why it is so dangerous to conduct your life from a place of want. That means desperation, and God's economy rewards like with like. Remember cause and effect? If you send desperation and need out into the universe, you will receive the same in return. "When we pray from the ego's fearful perception of lack, sickness, friction, and failure," wrote John Randolph Price, "we are affirming that we have not—and 'he that hath not, from him shall be taken even that which he hath.'"

Being in alignment with Spirit means finding the facts of your being. Who are you? What are you? What were you meant to achieve? What are you called to do in this life? You must figure out what your destiny is and then give everything you have to achieve it. Save nothing for a rainy day. God wants you to cast aside everything else that you have relied upon and lean completely on His laws. Your ability to do this will determine what you experience in the hereafter, because you cannot take material possessions with you, only your character. You don't see hearses with luggage racks. All you can take is your fully realized Spirit and your harmonized consciousness. They will create your next life as they create your current life.

You must figure out what your destiny is and then give everything you have to achieve it.

◯ ◯ ◯

Unite With God

In the end, what I am asking you to do is to begin moving toward a conscious union with God. Do not be in a supplicant position on your knees, as the churches would counsel, but a union as Father and child— not quite equal but of equal importance. Neither can achieve cherished goals without the other. That is truly your role in the cosmos. Now you are coming into some understanding of the true nature of God and yourself, and you can being to see that such a union is possible. Indeed, it is much to be desired. Joel S. Goldsmith wrote, "One individual having the spiritual understanding of the nature of God becomes a law of harmony, health, and supply unto thousands and thousands of people all over the world."

When you immerse yourself in the Laws of Being and become your fully aware "I Am" declaration that shapes your world, you are in union with God. Your mind becomes what it was always meant to be: an instrument that God uses to bring about harmony in the world according to His designs. That is why God created each and every one of us: to bring harmony to our fellows and heal the world. But because we have free will, we much each choose to follow or ignore this destiny. This is why some men are leaders and entrepreneurs and healers while others waste their lives with drugs, crime or selfishness. You are a tool, wielded by God's right hand, for bringing greater harmony to the universe—for pulling part of the cosmos out of chaos and entropy into order and beauty!

God is to be found only in the individual consciousnesses of each man and woman on this earth.

☉ ☉ ☉

So cease looking for God in the church. He's not there. Quit looking for Him in the Bible. He doesn't live between pages. Stop calling His name in fear and apprehension, because He doesn't listen. God is to be found only in the individual consciousnesses of each man and woman on this earth. God is pure Spirit. He cannot interact with this material plane directly, but He can interact with our conscious minds, because they are based on Spirit, as He is. So God in this world is not without, but *within*. That is a complete reinvention of what you have been told:

ↄ ↄ ↄ

GOD IS WITHIN YOU!

ↄ ↄ ↄ

It is your responsibility to develop your consciousness to fully unite with God in your mind and then in your actions. Mind becomes action. Thoughts shape the world. Your duty is to develop the consciousness of "IS," not "will be." God does not aspire; he simply states that something "IS." God is ever-present action. God is that which is aspired to already realized. *You have this same power.* You are a co-creator. Begin to think in terms of what you want already achieved and your Divine consciousness will bring it into existence. That is what God desires for you.

4

— THE LAW OF PROSPERITY —

ꝺ ꝺ ꝺ

All prosperity begins in the mind and is dependent only on the full use of our creative imagination.

—*Ruth Ross, historian*

We spend so much of our time on this earth musing, worrying and obsessing about money. It's a modern addiction, the concern over money. How can we get more of it? How can we save it? How should we use it? Do we even know what money really is? Hint: it's not pieces of paper with dead presidents on them. Author Ayn Rand put the question very well: "So you think that money is the root of all evil. Have you ever asked what is the root of all money?" Let's examine this question in this chapter and see if we can come to a realization of the true meaning of prosperity.

Money, as we said earlier, is the energy of change made material. Consider the chain of logic inherent in this: Man is God's agent of change on earth, money moves Man to focus attention on new things, this attention produces action, and action creates change— new businesses, new creative works, new political regimes. But where does money come from? Money, it turns out, comes from the Mind of God. But the ATM is not easy to access; its card does not come in the form of endless work or scrimping and saving.

You Are Infinite Plenty

Ralph Waldo Trine wrote, "This is the Spirit of Infinite Plenty, the Power that has brought, that is continually bringing, all things into expression in material form. He who lives in the realization of his oneness with this Infinite Power becomes a magnet to attract to himself a continual supply of whatsoever things he desires." You have the secret to prosperity within your Spirit: your willingness to make what you want come into being through your thoughts. That is the spirit of infinite prosperity, and it resides in each man and woman, though few figure out how to use it.

Prosperity is proof that you are excelling in living by His Laws and using His system.

ᓂ ᓂ ᓂ

Prosperity comes when you abandon the modern obsessing with earning paper money and stashing it in a bank account and understand that you ARE money—you make money come to you and manifest from the universe by trusting God's economy for all your needs. Think of the loaves and fishes. Jesus didn't hedge his bets by rounding up a few bakers and fishermen just in case His miracle didn't work, did he? Of course not! He gave Himself over completely to God's economy of plenty, knowing that only by surrendering all normal material thoughts of abundance could He call forth abundance from the cosmos. And so that meager amount of food fed a multitude.

Psalm 35:27 reads, "Let them shout for joy and rejoice, who favor my vindication; and let them say continually, 'The Lord be magnified, who delights in the prosperity of His servant.' " You read that right. God does not want you to take a vow of poverty. He wants you to be prosperous! Prosperity is proof that you are excelling in living by His Laws and using His system. The Kingdom of God is not a place, but a System in which your Mind is at one with the infinite Mind of God. When you live in that state at all times, prosperity will fill your hands with riches. Prosperity is a state of Spirit, and that Spirit is expressed in material wealth. If you want riches, quit saving and working harder and start seeing wealth coming to you in your Divine Mind.

The Power of Ideas

I'm not talking about the power of ideas to move men's hearts and change the world, though that is also an incredible aspect of the power of the idea. No, in our discussion the idea is the currency of God's economy. It is like a seed planted in the earth and left to grow. When you have an idea and send it out into the universe, it has causal power. An idea is far more than a firing of neurons in your brain; it is a Force. That idea flows into the cosmos, where it reacts with the essence of that cosmos that was formed from God's thought and so responds to mental declaration, the "I Am." These ideas set into motion subtle, titanic forces that slowly move the idea toward material manifestation. An idea is like a crucial stone pulled from an earthen dam. Imperceptibly, one stone starts a cascade that eventually breaches the dam and unleashes a flood—in this case, a flood of manifestation on the physical plane.

> *An idea is far more than a firing of neurons in your brain; it is a Force.*

You can imagine, then, how the idea of money and plenty can set in motion events that will bring money and plenty into your life. But to make this happen, you must first focus your attention on ideas that have the potential to bring good things into your orbit. This will always bring greater results than the limited approach that springs from want. Consider: you need more money to be able to afford to buy a home. You could choose to focus on what you need, essentially telling God's economy, "I do not have enough." But when you do this, you are broadcasting want and lack into the cosmos, and the cosmos will set that idea in motion. Want and lack will come back into your life again, and you will be where you started.

Or you could declare that your goal is already achieved and the money for the home is already in your bank account. Truly believing this sets in motion a different set of wheels that reflects the *plenty* in your thoughts and brings plenty to you. Do not be surprised if a sudden windfall or promotion gives you what you need to make that home a reality. That is the hidden power of ideas. Ideas and Spirit move God's economy, not dollars and cents.

Empty Yourself So You May Be Filled

One of the most counterintuitive aspects of the Law of Prosperity is the idea that you must cast away your means of support and create a vacuum in yourself in order for creation to fill it. The widow woman of Zarephath is a story that illustrates this principle beautifully. When Elijah came to her, she had nothing, yet he asked her to find food and water to sustain him. She had to empty all that she had in order for God to fill her pot of flour so she could bake bread. In other words, God can only work to bring plenty into your personal economy when you empty yourself of all other visible means of support and lean only on Him.

This can seem frightening, especially if you are in debt. How could you quit your job or give away your possessions and hope that God will bring a miracle into your awareness that will enable you to have what you need and more? This is an act of faith, and it is what God expects and demands of you in order for you to fulfill your destiny as a co-creator in the universe. You must clean out what is inside you that is not Spirit to make room for what you truly desire.

That's why giving is such a cleansing act. When you give away clothes or shoes that don't fit, when you divest yourself of your possessions, you are making room for God to bring new riches into your sphere.

This is the Vacuum Law of Prosperity. You must make that leap of faith and empty yourself of dependency, reliance on the limited and material, and thoughts of want and absence before God can begin to work. God wants you to give away your illusory means of support and rely only on His economy for your prosperity. As Catherine Ponder wrote in *The Dynamic Laws of Prosperity,* "You have heard it said that Nature abhors a vacuum. It is particularly true in the realm of prosperity. The vacuum law of prosperity is one of the most powerful, though it takes bold, daring faith to set it into operation, as well as a sense of adventure and expectation to reap its full benefits. When a person is honestly trying to be prosperous, is thinking along prosperous lines and still fails, it is usually because he needs to invoke the vacuum law of prosperity."

> *You must clean out what is inside you that is not Spirit to make room for what you truly desire.*

The Flow of Abundance

How wonderful to realize that riches and plenty are not dictated by the job you have or the education you've received, but by your thoughts! When you alter your consciousness to dwell in the plenty that you desire, you are diverting part of the river of Spirit energy that fills creation to bring substance to you, like water flowing through a river tributary. In this way, you can change your life by changing your thinking one thought at a time.

> *...you can change your life by changing your thinking one thought at a time.*
>
> ☾ ☾ ☾

The substance of material wealth—cars, cash, homes, jewelry—is not made of matter. It is energy that is given material form in order to exist on this plane, and as energy it is governed by the power of the Mind, not the power of the bank account. As Eric Butterworth writes, "The starting point in changing your life from financial reverses to an experience of abundance is the realization that you can change your life by altering your thoughts."

However, this paradigm shift from a focus on need and want ("I don't have enough money, so I need to earn more of it") to a Spirit-centered focus on bringing prosperity into existence by evolved thinking ("I am money, and I already have all the wealth I will ever need") only becomes possible when you know and can leverage the principles that govern prosperity. Let's take a closer look at those next.

The Compensation Principles

Just as in mathematics, music and the sciences, prosperity has rules, axioms and theorems that guide its flow and application. Only if you follow these rules can you fully realize the plenty and prosperity that God's System makes possible. They are called different things in different disciplines: cause and effect, action and reaction, supply and demand. But no matter what the name, the concept remains the same: you must give and divest yourself of the material crutches in your life in order to set God's economy in motion for your future. As the making and perception of patterns is a fundamental act of the conscious mind (think at how good humans are at picking a pattern out of almost any situation), the pattern of giving to receive must become the dominant pattern of your days.

One vital principle is that of giving God His due. This is the origin of the idea of tithing, giving 10% of your income to the church. Yes, this money is important to the material support of your church, but that is merely a side effect of this principle. Tithing is really a way for you to give to God what God deserves for all He has given you. The more you give away, the more you will get back! When you tithe beyond 10%, you are showing God that yes, you can surrender to His economy and turn your back on the limited material wealth

> *The more you give away, the more you will get back!*
>
> ☾ ☾ ☾

that we all worry so much about. When you can do this, you open the floodgates for unlimited wealth to flow your way, set in motion by your thought and awareness of your own Divinity. The Divine does not need money; the Divine only needs Spirit. Think and live thusly and you will be rich beyond measure.

On the opposite end of the spectrum you will find those who know chronic lack. They are always short a few dollars, aren't they? Always scrambling, praying and wishing for more money. If you experience times of want or know someone who is going through such a period, the reason is the same: you or they are denying God His due. As Achan does in Leviticus 27:32, you are robbing God of what is His and therefore stopping the flow of God's economy to yourself. Good withheld is a sign that you have not given something you should give. When your mother told you that you "have to give in order to receive," she knew what she was talking about! Amen.

The Rule of Compensation

Giving and the shedding of dependence on narrow materialistic wealth lie at the heart of the Laws of Being. This is because of the Rule of Compensation:

○ ○ ○

YOU CANNOT GET SOMETHING FOR NOTHING.

○ ○ ○

You could also phrase this as, "You get what you pay for." How true is that? How often have you bought something you needed at the cheapest price possible, maybe down at the local Wal-Mart, only to have it break down in a few days? Did you really save money? Or by trying to save money and buying something made in China, did you end up spending more on a replacement, gasoline, inconvenience and frustration? What if you had decided to spend more on the same product, but made by someone in the community? You would likely have been out of pocket a bit more, but your purchase would have lasted for years.

The rule of compensation makes it so that you can only get from God's economy what you pay for—you must give in equal measure to what you wish to receive. The more you send your possessions and money out into the world to work their energy for you, the more you will receive in return—opportunities, good people, windfalls, profitable ideas, incredible coincidences and more. The more you give, the more you lean on the economy of the Spirit for your means of living, and the more Spirit will reward you by setting events in motion to bring your desire into your sensory perception. What you want already exists in the etheric realm; your thoughts and your giving pay the price to bring what you want into material existence. When you give little and hoard what little you have, you are bypassing your good. To achieve prosperity, you must always follow these steps:

1. Give selflessly.

2. Rely on your "I Am," your declared faith that God has already given you what you need to be wealthy, for your sole support.

3. Gradually watch events turn in your favor and good come to you in many forms, multiplying your wealth many times over what you gave away.

Thanksgiving is the Cause, Plenty the Effect

Moses was called the Lawgiver because he understood the Laws of Being as few men ever have. In fact, he constantly pointed out the basic law of cause and effect to his followers. Moses knew God's economy; he had placed his faith in it as a means to thrown down the Egyptian domination of the Hebrews, which by any sane measure was impossible. But by casting aside any thought of rebellion and trusting God, Moses had been able to deliver his people. He knew the same applied to prosperity.

As Moses was aware, the act of thanksgiving is the key that opens the safety deposit box of God's cosmic bank account. No, I'm not speaking of the kind of thanksgiving that comes with turkey and mashed potatoes, but the act of giving thanks to God. But there's a catch. In the world of men, we thank someone after they have given us something. But in the economy of Spirit, thoughts have all the causal power. Your thoughts bring into being what you desire. So in order to "open the door for the more," you must give thanks to God *before* there is something in your material perception to give thanks for.

Say that again? You might be thinking, "Bishop, have you been spending too much time in the sun?" Bear with me. Remember that we attract only want when we think from a place of want. Like calls to like and the seed of lack and need will only bear the fruit of lack and need. We must approach the etheric energies from an attitude that what we wish is already achieved, so that we are thinking and believing from a place of plenty and abundance? Do you see? When you thank God for granting you that which does not yet exist in material reality, your sense of thanks and plenty set those energies in motion that bring that plenty to you. In days, weeks or months, you will see it. It is a law of nature as true as the fact that warm air rises. Thanksgiving rises and accelerates the process of prosperity, releasing the true power of your Mind. Think of gratitude as the secret ingredient in this thanksgiving dinner.

When you praise God for your good fortune to come, you unlock the doors.

☾ ☾ ☾

Now you understand the main reason for going to church and praising God. It's not because God is vain or egotistical. It's not because He will cast you into perdition if you don't praise Him. Those are outmoded ideas. The reason for praising God is because praise is the most powerful mode of thanks there is. The doors to prosperity have locks and keys, and praise is the most potent key for starting the flow of abundance. When you praise God for your good fortune to come, you unlock the doors. As Catherine Ponder writes in *The Millionaire Moses,* "The deliberate act of thanks liberates certain potent energies of mind and body that are not otherwise released. The deliberate act of thanksgiving can completely transform my life."

Mystic River

When you grasp and can make use of the laws and principles that underlie prosperity, you discover that wealth and plenty are at their core not goals but *mystical* processes. Follow the example of Melchizedek, who was a mystical millionaire, and Abraham, who also became fabulously wealthy as a result of his complete abdication of all means of wealth save trust in God. When you can use these principles and laws to their fullest, then prosperity becomes an automatic process, a mystical channel of wealth that operates on your behalf 24 hours a day, seven days a week.

This is where science and the mystical collide once again. You've heard many people talk about the Law of Attraction. Because of the bestseller *The Secret,* it's big business. But what the authors don't tell you is that simply thinking pretty thoughts isn't enough to bring true riches into your orbit. You must follow the Laws of Being, the laws of God's economy. Today, it's common to hear physicists talk about reality in mystical terms using words like "mind," "consciousness" and "oneness." This is a revolution; they are acknowledging what Western spiritual leaders and Eastern mystics have always known: the cosmos is based on the Mind. The Mind is the key to unlocking all its hidden doors and effects. Finally, disciplines are converging.

The road from poverty to affluence is paved with giving and the complete surrender to God's system. That is the only path to lasting wealth and plenty that makes a difference in your life and the lives of others. When something is lacking in your life, that is a sure sign that you are not giving enough. So you must spring into action: tithing to your church, giving away goods to the needy, giving of your time for a worthy cause. All of us have something worth giving. That act sets the mystical wheels of the cosmos turning and brings gifts back to you in proportion to what you give.

The Offering

Catherine Ponder writes, "Before embarking on a journey, going into battle, or facing any challenging situation, the Hebrews gave 'faith offerings' to their priests and temples in the faith that their mission would be successful. After returning from any challenging experience, they went directly to the priest or temple, and gave a 'thanks offering' in appreciation for the blessings received, and in order to 'seal' their new good and make it permanent."

Constant giving opens the way to constant receiving;

As you begin to grasp the importance of giving and thanks as the currency of the Divine economy, it is important that you also learn the finer mechanics of using them. One of these is the dual system of the "faith offering" and the "thanks offering." As illustrated in Ms. Ponder's passage, the faith offering is made in anticipation of great good to come, as a way of setting the machinery working in Spirit to bring wealth into physical reality. So when you have a great goal in mind, give something prior to setting out to achieve it so you will start the energy flowing. When it is achieved, give another gift in thanks to seal the good fortune and ensure that good things continue flowing toward you from the future to the present.

You can see that tithing is elevated to the status of a mystical law. Constant giving opens the way to constant receiving; indeed, it is the only path to a continual flow of positive energy, prosperity, ideas, opportunities and fruitful people in your life. Abraham tithed consistently to make way for receiving abundance from God just as consistently. It is as if there is only so much mystical room in our universe bank accounts, and until we clear space we cannot receive the riches of anointing from that universe. For most people, the call to tithe in this way comes only after a revelation from God (but that can be costly). God's revelations do not come on anyone's schedule but God's, so while you wait for a Divine revelation as your cue to start tithing before and after a major life goal, you might waste years not acting according to the Law of Prosperity.

Fortunately, you do not need a revelation. You have this book, which is a revelation it itself, albeit one that you can make notes in and re-read at your leisure to absorb more of its lessons.

The Law is Always Working

Giving is not optional in God's economy; it is mandatory. The Law of Prosperity is never NOT working; it either works for you or against you depending on how much you have given and how much you have made thanksgiving. To put it another way:

೧ ೧ ೧

YOU WILL EITHER GIVE VOLUNTARILY
OR INVOLUNTARILY.

೧ ೧ ೧

Voluntary giving turns the key in the lock of the universe's energy system and begins a flow in your direction. Nature abhors a vacuum, so when you empty yourself the universe will fill you and much more. Voluntary giving is an acknowledgement to God that you understand and accept His system. Involuntary giving goes under another name: debt. When you are miserly in your praise and tight-fisted in your giving, debt will grow in your fields where you once planted the hopes of wealth. Then you will find yourself giving in ways that are not so pleasing: bills, bankruptcy, gambling, perhaps a job loss. This is a destructive form of giving that serves no one and brings only ruinous experiences with it. But it's just the Law acting as God made it!

Understand that giving and thankfulness are key forces at work in your life every moment.

୨ ୨ ୨

You must not treat giving and thankfulness as actions to be chosen by conscious decision. This makes them seem optional. They are not. Giving and receiving is a universal cycle that plays out throughout the cosmos. The seas give water so that rain may fall on crops. Plants give their lives and the energy they harvest from the sun so that animals may live. Doctors, police and teachers give of their time so that people can receive health, safety or learning. Every day, all around you, giving and receiving are going on. EXPECT THEM! Understand that giving and thankfulness are key forces at work in your life every moment. They are always at work giving you what you ask for, whether you know you're asking for it or not.

What Are You Preparing For?

Florence Scovel Shinn writes, "If one asks for success and prepares for failure, he will get the situation he has prepared for." You are always preparing for something. We all are. Some of us are aware of it and can change our thoughts and faith actively so that what we prepare for will be what we receive. Others are ignorant of their own preparation, so that they are subject to the whims and tides of life and never receive what God has ordained. In which camp would you prefer to be? In which camp have you been until reading this book?

You are the creator and maker of your thoughts. God has given you a Mind sprung from His Mind, and that Mind wields the power to shape and alter the cosmos, if you will utilize it. But as Ernest Holmes said, it is a conscious and ongoing process: disciplining your mind and your belief, creating new patterns of thinking and self-awareness and traveling in the patterns of those thoughts, evolving your Mind to the point where consciously and unconsciously, you are living the "I Am" awareness that makes your desire manifest in your mind and brings it to you in the material.

When this inner alchemy—transmuting thought and mystical giving into abundance, opportunity and creation in the physical plane—becomes not a decision but part of who you are, you will be living the Law of Prosperity to the utmost.

5

— THE LAW OF COMPENSATION —

೧ ೧ ೧

If we will be quiet and ready enough, we shall find compensation in every disappointment.

—*Henry David Thoreau*

In Ecclesiastes, we read, "To everything there is a season, and a time to every purpose under Heaven." We also find, "He has made everything beautiful in its time. He has also set eternity in the hearts of men; yet they cannot fathom what God has done from beginning to end." What do these passages mean and what do they have to do with one another? The first clearly references the idea that each event in life must happen in its own due time; it cannot be rushed or moved by man, but must obey the laws that God has set down. Even God must obey His own laws.

The second is more subtle. It means that in its proper context, everything is a blessing. The loss of something you hold dear may not appear to be a blessing at the time, but given enough time and as the workings of God's laws play out, the result of that loss will turn out to be a greater benefit to you than what you gave up. As we often see, the hardest times of our lives—divorce, job loss, health crisis, conflicts with friends, money problems—turn out to be the greatest blessings because in those challenges we find greater strength discover new things about ourselves, and find new paths to walk through life. That is the essence of these ideas and the heart of the Law of Compensation.

Every Act Has a Sequence

In his seminal book *The Science of Mind,* Ernest Holmes wrote, "Jesus said, 'Give and to you shall be given.' All the great scriptures have announced this central and transcendent truth, realizing that every act carries with it a sequence, bringing the result of this action back to the self." This means that for every act we engage in, no matter how small or supposedly unseen, there is compensation in kind from the universe, as long as we can wait for the proper sequence of events to play out.

Pay out misery and you're going to get misery plus one back in your life.

So if someone were to perform a dishonest act that cost a friend's business an important customer, that act would eventually boomerang on the one who committed it, but not right away. Let's say the business was seasonal. The person who performed the dishonest deed might not see the compensation for his deed for months, but when the appropriate season came around—BOOM. He would receive the same injury he visited upon his neighbor, only greater. You could call this God's interest. Pay out misery and you're going to get misery plus one back in your life. Pay out charity, goodness and prosperity and you will receive them all back enhanced and enlarged.

So everything you lose, you gain back, positive and negative. Really, you can never lose anything forever. What is yours is always yours. You will always experience the consequences of your actions in some way. When you give with no thought of what you will receive in return, you will receive much, because your mind is focused only on the plenty that you are creating for others. When you give grudgingly, you will eventually receive meager reward. That's what you buy. The upshot is that you must learn to lose *gracefully*. You will lose things and opportunities, but you must lose them with the understanding that the loss is part of God's natural cycle of seasons, and you will get them back in time, but only if you can lose them with grace, welcoming the loss. Notice the double meaning of "grace" here: the meaning we're used to, *undeserved favor from God,* and the act of losing with an open heart and a positive attitude. Both are vital.

When you understand that for everything you lose you gain something, you can invoke the law of Divine Restoration in your life to guide you through dark times. As Catherine Ponder writes, "Stop dwelling on apparent losses in your life, and start looking for the growth and gain that came through them. For every loss there has been a gain, so drop the loss and take the gain!"

Every Day is a Season

With this knowledge, you can see that God has ordained seasons for loss and seasons for compensation. But you have no way of knowing which seasons come at which times, for there is a different cycle of seasons for human and each area of his or her earthly life: a job season, a money season, a relationship season, a house season, a health season, a child season, a faith season, a war season and many others. But since you have no way to know when a season is coming to pass, every day is a day of compensation, a day when you may either sow the seeds or reap the harvest of some thought or action.

As Eric Butterworth writes, "You must choose each day to oppose God's laws or to abide by them." Whatever choice you make, you will reap the results of the unstoppable Law of Compensation. Your choices will bear fruit regardless. This results in a truth that is hard for some to fathom, but true nevertheless:

○ ○ ○

WE ARE NOT PUNISHED FOR OUR SINS, BUT BY OUR SINS.

○ ○ ○

God does not pour wrath on our heads like some bad version of the Old Testament. No, He has created the Law of Compensation to operate as a sort of automatic reward and punishment system. If we do ill, ill will be our reward. If we do good and live according to the Laws of Being, we will enjoy prosperity and blessings.

If this sounds suspiciously like the Hindu concept of karma, you're right. It is the same thing. Do not disregard the ancient wisdom of other cultures because they are non-Christian; all faiths are but different inter-pretations of the same eternal truths. The idea that "what goes around comes around" is central to many cultures, but few comprehend it as the result of the Law of Compensation. You also know the principle as the Golden Rule: what you do to others comes back to you. Jesus said, "Whatsoever you do to the least of my brothers, that you do unto me." This is the basis for all systems of law and morality—the concept that inexorably, our thoughts and actions will always be reflected back upon us. There is no escape.

The Power of Prayer

For centuries, the faithful have misunderstood the nature of prayer. They have mistaken it for some sort of broadband phone line to God on which they could ask the Almighty to intervene in daily affairs. But that is incorrect. God does not interfere in our lives; He lets His laws work their wonders for better or worse. Prayer only works in concert with the Law of Compensation. You cannot get something for nothing. Prayer does not dissolve debts or erase guilt; it sets the wheels of compensation in motion. When you pray, you offer up to God your faith in His system, and His laws reward you appropriately. That is why you cannot pray effectively when you do not fully comprehend the Laws of Being. Without this knowledge, you cannot pray without an offering, and it is unlawful to pray without one. You oppose God's laws when you do so, and you will receive nothing in return.

> *Prayer only works in concert with the Law of Compensation.*
>
> ☙ ☙ ☙

Prayer results in judgment, but again, this is a misunderstood term. God does not judge His children; our own actions pass judgment on us and hand down reward or penalty. Obey the laws of God and judgment will be in your favor, setting positive events in motion and giving you more than you gave. Defy the laws and judgment will be harsh and rob you of even more than you thought you had already lost. "Every defect in one manner is made up in another. Every suffering is rewarded; every sacrifice is made up; every debt is paid," wrote Ralph Waldo Emerson.

Every Thought Yields a Harvest

You must see your very thoughts as seeds, and the cosmos as the soil in which those seeds are sown. The farmer sowing seeds of corn in his fields cannot resist the pull of gravity that draws his seed downward into the earth, once there, to germinate and produce a crop according to the conditions and their kind. So can you not resist the harvest nature of reality; you are always sowing some kind of crop. Every one of your thoughts will produce a result of some kind, positive or negative. Thoughts are a pendulum that swings outward as the thought takes shape in your mind and projects outward, then swings back to you with the same kind of energy you used to project it out. What your thoughts sow, you shall reap: hate for hate, courage for courage, love for love.

The cosmos must remain in balance, and so what you desire must be paid for with something of equal price.

Just as the Law of Compensation guarantees that each thought will produce a harvest, so too does it guarantee that nothing comes without a price. The cosmos must remain in balance, and so what you desire must be paid for with something of equal price. If you desire health in someone you love, that health may be bought with a health problem of your own, developed while you strained to care for the loved one with the initial health crisis. Nothing is free; even God cannot change His law in this area. You must always give something up in order to gain something, and you will usually know what that something is—it is whatever blocks you from depending entirely on God for your means of support and succor.

In this equation of personal and universal economy, like attracts like. You must understand and live by this principle if you are to benefit from it and live in harmony with God's system. What you project into the etheric plane—whether it is thought, faith, declaration or a gift to another—will return to you in the same form. Gift will yield gift, sorrow will yield sorrow, wealth will return wealth. Science reflects this same concept in the laws of thermodynamics. The first law says that energy may never be created or destroyed; it can only be changed. God respects this law, but He has named it differently as the Law of Compensation. There is nothing new under the sun. What you give cannot change form, for that is a violation of Law. It must return to you in the same form, either magnified or diminished. In this way do we create our own futures, our own judgment, even our own punishment!

No Free Lunch

God has given us all so much: life and Law, love and possibility, as well as a role as His regents on this material plane. But He asks something in return. He asks that we pay His price for what we want, and that is living and acting according to His system. You dare not try to get something for nothing, and you dare not take shortcuts to try to get what you desire. If you ask God for something from a place of nothing, nothing is what you will receive. Words are meaningless; it is the faith behind them that matters. Remember, you can never get rich coming from a position of need and want. You must give God what He demands from each of us before you can receive.

> *Words are meaningless; it is the faith behind them that matters.*

What does God demand? What is this pearl of great price? *Generosity of spirit.* You must give of yourself, your time, your money, your love, your expertise, some part of you must be given away with a true heart in order to put God's laws into action. Remember action and reaction? In space flight, rocket fuel shoots out the bottom of a rocket in a gout of flame. It annihilates everything in its path, but at the same time it provides the thrust to propel the vessel into the air and to "slip the surly bonds of earth." Your initial action can be as misunderstood as the flaming fuel, which in another context would be nothing more than a destructive conflagration. But God's laws perceive it as a gift and reward it.

There is no way around this infrastructure of human desire. As I said, there are no shortcuts. You cannot receive before you give. You must follow the sequence and wait for the season. You must give or think with a total surrender to God's economy. Then you must allow time to pass and the hidden machinery of reality to work in your favor. Only then can you begin to see the results of your embrace of the Law of Compensation. It will be hard to have less while others are wallowing in their riches from having embraced easy paths and lower ideals, but you must endure. In the end, God will bless all who Obey His laws and send the rest nothing but confusion.

> *You cannot receive before you give.*
>
> ☾ ☾ ☾

No Free Lunch, Part 2

Have you ever noticed that when your fortunes change, so do the people in your life? New people arrive and others fade away? This is not accidental, but yet another face of the Law of Compensation. When you give of yourself in a spirit of generosity and plenty, you will receive the same in return in greater measure. But you will lose something as well. As James Allen wrote, "Gain in a given direction necessitates loss in its opposite direction. The force placed in one scale is deducted from the other scale." In all things, there must always be balance: in your life, your relationships, your health and in the universe. God maintains that balance through His laws.

For instance, if you become wealthy, you will change your friends. Hangers-on who only want to be around you as parasites will quickly give way to more accomplished friends who truly care about you and can help you reach your goals. Those old friends were a loss necessary to retain the balance of energy in the universe. You will always lose something when you gain. The exercise of Law always requires a sacrifice. Frequently, this sacrifice will be a part of yourself that you would be better off without. As James Allen wrote, "Selfish pleasure must be sacrificed if purity is to be gained; hatred must be yielded up if love is to be acquired; vice must be renounced if virtue is to be embraced." You are required to sacrifice a vice on the altar of virtue if you are to bring blessings into your experience. Like it or not, God is working through His laws to help you become a more aware, healthier, more peace-loving, intellectually rich individual.

God's Dice Are Always Loaded

In *The Infinite Way,* Joel Goldsmith writes, "As we learn to listen for that 'still small voice' which spoke to Elijah, we, too, will be led to where our work and recognition and compensation are to be found. We exist as individual Consciousness; therefore, all that is necessary to our fulfillment is included in the infinite Consciousness which we are." It should be clear to you by this time that every one of your thoughts calls forth compensation from the cosmic Consciousness. Everything you do and are is answered by God's Laws. So you need not ever worry that your good works or your giving that seem to go unnoticed by others are truly going unnoticed. They are setting forces in motion that will deliver to you compensation in like kind. Good yields good.

So no one who is educated in the nature and substance of the Law of Compensation ever need worry about having the means of support, love, happiness or creation. You are the means. The creative seed for all that you need resides in your limitless Mind, the key that turns the tumblers and levers of the economic system of the universe. Supply is within you and will flow out to meet demand, provided that you fully embrace that you are the supply and that your thoughts produce that which you demand. If by your thoughts you demand scarcity, ill will or sickness, that it what your Consciousness will supply. If you demand wealth and health, so too will your Consciousness comply.

> *The creative seed for all that you need resides in your limitless Mind,*

This reality is God's responsibility to us. He is our Creator, and as such He has the duty to give us the means to survive and thrive, just as a parent has the duty to impart to his children the knowledge and morals they will need. Note that this does not imply dependency; God is not going to intervene in your life if you make foolish choices and bail you out. Again, a wise parent will not bail his child out of a bad situation, because only through such experiences do we learn. So, too, does God give us all we need to have abundant supply, but relies on our wisdom to discover the path to that supply. That's not the arrangement. God supplies you with the means, the System, to create great riches, prosperity, health and joy in your existence as long as you remember that He is the source and live in harmony with His laws.

As Goldsmith says, "God's dice are always loaded." That means that God always shows favor to those who understand and live by His laws. You may experience temporary reversals in this world, but as long as you remember God and tune your mind to the Laws of Being, being the Divine co-creator that you are, you cannot remain down for long. God System of reward will always lift you up.

Now, the Bad News

There is always a catch, isn't there? It's an obvious one. As you can doubtless see, the Law of Compensation is without morality. It simply responds to whatever thought or faith you project into the cosmos. So in the same way that right thought will produce true, beneficial results, wrong thoughts will curse you with misfortune. If you abuse God's laws, you will find yourself on the receiving end of anything from financial difficulties to health problems to

...the Law of Compensation is without morality.

betrayal by trusted friends. You never know when "what goes around comes around" will come around to lay you low!

For this reason, you should never borrow money from a friend. It changes the dynamic of the relationship. Suddenly, one of you is indebted to the other, and the lender is placed in a superior position. This alters the vibrations you both send out into the etheric plane and affects how the Law of Compensation reacts to you. As a borrower, you are broadcasting your need into the universe, so what do you think the universe will pay you back with? That's right, need. So when the time comes to repay the loan, you won't have the money. It is better to delay gratification and try to get what you need through patience, sacrifice and right thought than to get something for nothing, inviting the impersonal backlash of the Law of Compensation. In a sense, Compensation is the High Chancellor of God, weighing out the payment of rewards and the collection of debts on a fine scale and determining who is worthy of each.

Writes Ponder, "When you are tempted to try to get something for nothing, remind yourself that you are only delaying your good. It must first be earned in the consciousness of your own thoughts and feelings before there can be any permanent outer result."

True Joy is the Finest Pay

So in the end, the Law of Compensation does not care about you individually. It is a harsh master, rewarding you in exactly the manner in which you use it. But since the Law responds to thought, it makes sense that true compensation begins where duty ends. In other words, when you live with joy and passion and the love of creation, you are setting in motion wonderful things for your future. That is why you should not engage in a job unless it gives you joy and fulfillment. A man who receives only a paycheck for his work is a poor man indeed.

So in the end, the Law of Compensation does not care about you individually.

I recognize that this is not always an option. Sometimes, you feel you must work to pay the bills and keep a roof over your head. But have you ever thought about the great inventors, artists, and entrepreneurs? They took great risks to follow their passionate vision to the disregard for monetary needs, and the universe responded to their passion. Look at the word "function." It's a combination of "fun and "unction," meaning anointing. If you don't have fun in your unction, you are not doing the right thing with your days. Do not spend yourself out of a sense of obligation or to satisfy what you think society expects to you do; use your days in a way that speaks to your Spirit, and that joy will call out to the Law of Compensation and create wonders.

> *...use your days in a way that speaks to your Spirit,*
>
> ○ ○ ○

A man I know told me about a friend of his who exemplifies this idea perfectly. She was a jazz singer who desperately wished she could be like the chanteuses of the 1940s who sang with their combos in clubs around Los Angeles. Inspired, she pulled together her own money, hired a jazz trio, and started her own weekend sessions at a classic Hollywood eatery. She never tried to commercialize the venture; she did it only for the love of it. But her passion rang out to the cosmos, and the cosmos responded. Word got out to recording professionals, who came to see her and eventually signed her to a contract with Blue Note. That is the power of doing something with all the joy and passion in your soul.

Give Yourself a Raise

It should be very clear by now: your compensation is entirely up to you. If it's not what you want, you can't blame God. If it's spectacular, give yourself a pat on the back for doing right. There is no chance. Everything that happens to you is the result of some thought or action that set off the Law of Compensation. Your individual actions will always determine your individual compensation. You will attract to yourself what you have chosen to receive by virtue of your Mind and your choices.

Some have taken umbrage with this idea by saying, "So you're saying that people who get cancer asked for it?" No, that is not the message. No one asks for disease. What we broadcast into the ether by our thoughts, actions and beliefs does come back to us in like form; however, we may have no idea what specific form that compensation will take. Ill breeds ill, but not necessarily a mirror image. So an immoral act might return a personal betrayal or the appearance of cancer, but it is the negative nature of the result that matters, not the specific form the result takes. So when people speak of accident and chance they are truly speaking out of ignorance.

What Will You Give Up?

The Law of Compensation depends on you. That can be a frightening idea, that there is an implacable force in the cosmos ready to revisit all our sins and good deeds on us in unknown ways at an unknown time in the future. But that is the way of things. Think of it this way: this reality gives you all the power you need to create a life of plenty and happiness for yourself and others. There's only one question you have to answer:

ʘ ʘ ʘ

WHAT ARE YOU GOING TO GIVE UP?

ʘ ʘ ʘ

In an essay, Ralph Waldo Emerson wrote that for everything you gain, you lose something. That is part of God's economy. You must surrender something in order to make room for the plenty that the Law of Compensation is planning to bring into your awareness. It's normal: at birth, you lose your umbilical cord to gain independent life. By reading this book, you have lost comforting illusions about God but gained a new realization of your power over your future. There is no gain without loss. The question is, do you have the wisdom to see what you no longer need and the courage to part with it?

In his seminal book *Think and Grow Rich,* Napoleon Hill wrote that each failure brings with it the seed of an equivalent advantage. In letting go of things that we thought we needed, we discover in ourselves the persistent strength to endure and the might to leverage the Law of Compensation—emptying ourselves so that God may fill us. That is the most enduring success of all.

6

— THE LAW OF FREEDOM —

꩜ ꩜ ꩜

None are so hopelessly enslaved as those who falsely believe they are free.

—*Johann Wolfgang von Goethe*

Are we really free? Or are we slaves of impulses we cannot control? Many of today's scientists would claim that free will is an illusion—that because we are (according to them) nothing more than complex collections of chemicals controlled by the laws of physics, all our actions are dictated by those laws and are therefore completely *deterministic*. Therefore, we have no free will. We are automatons who simply cherish the delusion that we are causal agents in the world.

But then you have things like the placebo effect, which you have probably heard about. The word *placebo* is Latin for "I will please," referring to a placebo's effect in satisfying the recipient's wishes. A placebo is an inert drug or other treatment that works because the patient expects it to work. Without belief, there can be no placebo. This effect is often discussed with disdain, but it's incredibly powerful.

Witness a real case from the literature in which a man with terminal cancer and days to live went to see his doctor to try to get a dose of a new drug that was still experimental. His doctor, figuring the man had nothing to lose, gave the man the drug. Immediately, the man's tumors began to shrink and had disappeared within weeks. Later, a news story revealed that the drug was ineffective, and when the man heard this, his cancer returned. His doctor, wishing to repeat the same powerful healing effect, told him that a newer version of the drug had been released and gave him an injection—*of water.* The man's tumors again vanished. Unfortunately, a medical journal article appeared a few months later that conclusively found that the drug was completely worthless, and when the patient found out about this information, he quickly became cancer-ridden again and died.

What does this mean for our discussion of freedom? Well, think about the meaning of the placebo effect. If, as the deterministic scientists feel, the body and brain are nothing more than chemicals and electrical signals firing according to physical laws, then there is no such thing as a mind working as a causal agent. The body directs thoughts, not the other way around. But if that is the case, how can the placebo effect, which depends on *belief,* work? According to the determinists, belief doesn't exist, so how can it have an effect on the body? How can a purely mental event produce incredible healing? The answer: we are more than chemicals and electrical impulses. Our minds are causal forces in the world. Free will is real.

Our minds are causal forces in the world.

ꙩ ꙩ ꙩ

Our Spiritual Inheritance

In John 8:32, the Bible says, "And ye shall know the truth, and the truth shall make you free." But what is the truth? It is that we are free from the beginning and that where the spirit of God dwells, there is freedom. We are free to pick and choose our own path from the choices God has laid before us. God has prepared the table and enabled us to make the choice, but we must choose what to eat. We are free in word and deed, but we must exercise caution, because our words and deeds define us. God's freedom is like a screenplay, which follows a very specific structure, but within that structure the writer is allowed limitless creativity. Within God's freedom, we can make infinite choices.

> *Within God's freedom, we can make infinite choices.*
>
> ◑ ◑ ◑

Bondage or freedom? Those are our choices, and only we can choose for ourselves. Bondage does not really exist in the sense that we know it: another party exercising power over us to limit our movements or freedom to act as we will. We can always act as we will. However, the choices we make can have the effect of limiting our freedom and therefore become bondage *in comparison* with the total freedom we have when we act in accordance with the Laws of Being. Reduced freedom is the same as bondage; when they were cast out from the Garden, Adam and Eve were still free to do as they pleased. But compared with the immortal bliss they had known in paradise, they were in a prison in which their live would only come from the toil of their hands and Eve would only bear children from pain.

Where the Spirit of God is, there is the potential of freedom. That is all that is needed for complete freedom—no money, power or health is needed as a prerequisite. God avails completely for freedom; He is the price of it. Freedom is your spiritual inheritance from the Lord.

Freedom to Do What?

This is a common question when I discuss the Law of Freedom. People ask if they are free from the common restrictions of morality and Christian teachings that they have held to for years. I say the same to them that I say to you now: you have always been free. The universe holds nothing against you. You are free in word and deed and not bound by any religious teachings or strictures from doing anything you wish, positive or negative. However, those teachings exist for a reason: religious and spiritual masters understand the other Laws and know that one's actions can affect one's freedom. Therefore, in choosing how to exercise your freedom, it is wise to act in ways that will not deny you freedom in your later life.

> *The universe holds nothing against you.*
>
> ා ා ා

For example, a basic teaching of Christianity is "Thou shalt not kill." If you chose to defy this Commandment and take someone's life, God would not stop you; you would remain free to exercise your free will and commit murder. However, that decision would doubtless cost you your freedom: you would be prosecuted and imprisoned. The other Laws of Being do not sit idly by as you exercise your freedom; they are always in effect and there are always consequences for actions. So while you can act with pure freedom, you should do so in a way that conforms to the other laws, so you don't set in motion reactions that will deny you freedom in the future.

Imagine that you stand on the roof of a 20-story building. Nothing prevents you from exercising the freedom to jump off, but if you do, the law of gravity will inevitably pull you to your death on the street below. The law bears you no ill will, but it must act as it has been designed to act, without exception. You flex your freedom and must pay the price exacted by the inviolable laws. So it is in the spiritual realm. You are free to say, act, create, love, build, fight, slander, cheat and steal as you like, but there is always a price to pay. As Ernest Holmes wrote, "The Law punishes us automatically until, through experience, we learn what is right and just, and then we are immediately forgiven."

The Nature of Bondage

You are not one of the Hebrews at the time of Moses, born into bondage to Egypt. Bondage does not exist in real terms; it is nothing more than a misuse of the Law of Freedom, the kind we discussed above. You are the prime mover of your destiny; you are the force acting on your own life. God has set the laws down and given you the means to use them, but He will not interfere with how you choose to act upon them. The only person who can work against you is you.

So when you feel that forces are arrayed against you, limiting your choices, you must ask yourself, "What have I done to limit my own freedom?" Think hard; deeds or words of many years past can be the catalyst for a loss of freedom, so it may take heroic introspection and feats of memory to find the culprit in your own past. Once you find it, you must ask another question: "Can I rectify the situation?" Can you repair the damage and regain all your freedom? This is a key question we all face as we pile up relationships, jobs, decisions and mistakes in our past. Life is like a computer's hard drive: when we take it out of the box, it's clean and pristine. As life goes along, the drive becomes cluttered with errors and corrupt files. Eventually, we cannot do what we want until we repair the damage, clean off the drive. This is the reason it is so vital to be mindful at all times how you are living the Laws.

Be Our Guest

You are a guest in this life, God's guest in His house, and as any gracious host does, He has placed many gifts and conveniences at your disposal. One of the greatest—perhaps the greatest—is free will. But what kind of guest are you? Are you hoarding your freedom and refusing to use it, or are you sharing it with the world? This returns us to the idea that God rewards those of us who live on the edge, who take risks and shed their common sense means of support to rely only on God's laws for sustenance—who spend 40 days fasting in the desert or trek across country with nothing but the clothes on their backs, relying on the kindness of others to sustain them.

In other words, exercise your freedom to do things that are bold, risky or even crazy.

☾ ☾ ☾

A vital aspect of the Law of Freedom is that you must be a grateful guest by giving of your freedom and using it to conform to the other Laws. In other words, exercise your freedom to do things that are bold, risky or even crazy. A man who does not use his God-given freedom to remake the world in some way is betraying the gift.

When you misuse your freedom, you place yourself in bondage. It is like being a guest in a fine home and never coming out of your room. You can see this in people who have decided that they cannot take even the smallest risks and who fear everything. Their lives are stunted and constrained. You also see this attitude in those who want to take a leap of faith but cannot seem to do it; they are always "waiting for something." They say they will take that big step "after the new year" or "when I get that raise." There's always an excuse. They are waiting for permission, for someone to grant them the freedom to act. But they have always had the freedom; no one need grant it to them. They have placed themselves in bondage by refusing to give their freedom back to the world. Remember:

○ ○ ○

BONDAGE IS ALWAYS SELF-INFLICTED.

○ ○ ○

Limitation is a misuse of the Law of Freedom. It can be the result of destructive patterns of thinking, or of a damaging decision made years before but that you have not taken action to correct. In any case, bondage is always optional. It can be ended with a single thought, a single word. Your term in prison is only as long as you choose it to be. You are your own jailer, and the Universe's Laws are your only judge.

Reverse Course!

In his book *Change Your Thinking, Change Your Life,* Ernest Holmes writes, "Undesirable conditions are themselves proof that we have injured ourselves by using the Law of Freedom in a limited way. We must now reverse our thinking, and for every negative thought we must supply an affirmative one. This is not as difficult as it seems to be, but calls for imagination and decision, not as will, but as willingness. We must affirm the Truth until we arrive at a state of consciousness which accepts our own affirmations." You are, of course, free to maintain any patterns of thought that you wish; that's part of Divine freedom. However, when you find that your limited use of freedom has effectively put you in bondage, the best and most effective way to escape is to actively reverse your thinking—to consciously train your mind to think in a different way.

I will illustrate. Let's say we have a man who has grown up deeply suspicious of all people, so much so that we could call him paranoid. He trusts no one, and so he has no real friends. He leads a lonely existence devoid of joy or love. He is in emotional bondage. Not only can he not enjoy the delight of a romantic relationship, but he has no one in his life with whom he can share his dreams, no one who can aid him in accomplishing his goals. He is an island. But as John Donne wrote, "No man is an island." Existing in this way is devastating to the spirit.

If this man wants to escape this state, what must he do? He must reverse course in his mind—begin to deliberately regard others as trustworthy, go out of his way to trust and confide in others. Only then will he begin to have that trust returned, as like breeds like. By reversing course in this way he will exceed those bitter limitations he had placed on himself and discover his greater freedom. This illustrates another truth:

◡ ◡ ◡

IT IS ONE THING TO HAVE FREEDOM, ANOTHER
TO HAVE THE WISDOM AND COURAGE
TO USE IT PROPERLY.

◡ ◡ ◡

Mind Control

The idea of mind control has negative implications. It reminds us of totalitarian societies and George Orwell's *1984*. But you can also regard this phrase in a positive way: control over your thoughts and your mind and the power they wield. As you know by now, all thought is creative. Not just creative in the sense of creating art or literature, but in the sense that thoughts exercise a causal power in the universe. Thoughts bring forth actions, events and consequences. Thoughts can set events in motion that you do not intend, and those events can wreak havoc on your life or the lives of others. The power of your mind is not to be taken idly. So as you have complete freedom to act as you will, so must you be mature enough to control your thoughts and channel them to do good. Bondage exists when you do not exercise control over your thoughts and they limit you.

Bondage exists when you do not exercise control over your thoughts and they limit you.

ᕫ ᕫ ᕫ

Every thought you have is a creation waiting to come into being. This is why many individuals who embrace deep spiritual truth often choose to live lives of contemplation and prayer: Christian and Buddhist monks, Hindu holy men, Islamic pilgrims and muezzins. They understand how vital it is to discipline your thoughts. That is also why I always correct people who scoff at those who choose a cloistered existence of prayer, meditation, silence and service as being "do nothings." They are not. They are deeply wise people who know that their ungoverned thoughts have the power to work evil in the world. They do us all a great service by controlling their thoughts. You should aspire to do the same, even if you don't run away to a monastery!

It should be clear by now that freedom is not doing whatever you like. It is *becoming what you were ordained to be by the mind of God.*

In John 8:32, Jesus said, "Ye shall know the truth and the truth shall make you free." But what was this freedom? It was the freedom to harness the spiritual truth within you and achieve your Divine destiny. Since the beginning, God has held in His mind a vision of who and what you could become. Deuteronomy 30:19 calls upon us to choose between blessings and curses and to choose wisely; this is clearly a choice of the way in which we will use our freedom to become that which God has ordained we should become.

Become the Law

As with so much in the realm of the Laws, this is about more than acting; it is about Being. Your entire life has been about the tension between God's perfect vision and your achievement of it. The more you deviate from the destiny that God has designed for you, the more you will find your life enmeshed in conflict, misfortune and anxiety. You will live as if you are swimming against the tide, because you are: the tide of God's intention.

It means that you must become the state of freedom that you wish to achieve...

Following the Law of Freedom means more than simply saying, "OK God, you win, I'll do what you want." That is subjugation, not freedom. God does not want you to become passive any more than we wants you to defy His vision for you. He wants you to become freedom in your consciousness—to become one with His ordained destiny. What does this mean? It means that you must become the state of freedom that you wish to achieve, act and think and feel as though your full destiny as already been achieved. When you do this, your consciousness becomes reality to those around you and to your world. Consciousness is the substrate of reality, not matter or energy. As physicists are discovering this, so are spiritualists. Consciousness is the ground state of all there is, stemming from God. So when your consciousness is tuned to the pitch of your perfect God-given destiny, that destiny will become realized.

But how can you know if you're tuned to that perfect good? You will know when you are aligned with the good you desire when you feel the limitless energy of God welling up within you, bursting to be expressed. Perfect freedom is the state of being at one with God's intent for you. As Eric Butterworth writes, "The will of God is the ceaseless longing of the Spirit in you to completely fulfill the outer the potential within you. The will of God in you is the pent-up energy of your own divinity that is seeking release and fulfillment in your life. It is God seeking to express Himself as you, as radiant health, as eternal youth, as an all sufficiency of supply, as freedom from limitation of any kind."

Remember that God created each one of us to express a tiny part of His infinite vision for the material plane. You are an individualized center of the Consciousness of God, who is Consciousness itself. You are of the essence of God. You are the sole custodian of one infinitesimal bit of His Divine vision. Finding your own way to fulfill it completely is why you were granted freedom in the first place. When you become conscious of the total good of your nature, evil and limitation disappear, as they did for Jesus.

Your Mind of God

It is assumed by many who are not enlightened that no one can know the Mind of God. This is untrue. How can you not know the Mind of God when you are part of that Mind? Your mind is one activity within the infinite Mind of the Creator, and when you speak, you speak with the Mind and Voice of God. Did you not wonder why your very words and thoughts have the power to bring things into being? Why people focusing their minds on "intention" can heal others from thousands of miles away? You think the thoughts of God; His Mind is the Law of your life.

Once you accept this, you can come to know the truth, which is that you are a Spirit walking in this life as flesh, brought into the material plane for one reason: to bring one miniscule piece of God's eternal vision into being. This is your true self, though there are many paths to this type of self-discovery. You might choose deep contemplation, sacrifice and suffering, hard work and toil, service to others, or some other path that makes sense to you. The nature of the path is not important; what matters is that you walk a path that leads you to this profound understanding of your true self.

When you reach this state, you will gain new eyes, and with them you will be able for the first time to see the falsehood of much of what you have thought to be important. Vanity, destructive actions, envy, rivalry, hoarding and greed—all are false gods, traitors to your true self. They will claim to be the truth of your life, but they will do nothing more than guide you away from your freedom, your true potential. Seeing your nature as an active participant in the Mind and Thought of God will empower you to see right through these pernicious illusions and reject them. You can cast them out as easily as Jesus cast the moneychangers from the temple.

The Paradox of Freedom

Once again, we come back to the enormity of your responsibility as one of God's regents in this material world. That is the reason He created the Law of Freedom and set it in motion, as well as all the other Laws of Being: there must be consequences for not following the destiny God has laid down for you. Think about it: how many human beings do you think have the wisdom, courage, humility, strength and vision to discover their true selves, become the Laws and bring their part of God's Vision to total fruition? Ten percent? Five percent?

What would the world be like if there were no Laws to confine and channel our energies and teach us when we stray from the intent of God? The world would be chaos and God's designs would rarely if ever reach fruition. What a hell that would be! In a way, we are bound by the Law of Freedom in a kind of bondage; the Law coerces us to act in a certain manner in order to achieve certain results in our lives. But this is not a bondage of limitations, but the very necessary consequence of living in a cosmos where order rules instead of chaos. Remember that once He set them into motion, even God was bound by His Laws. He cannot violate them without undoing everything that was created by them. This is the reason that God also will not intervene in your life other than to inspire you, speak to you in prayer or meditation or send you signs or visions. God is a God of *information* and *inspiration*, not intervention.

> *Remember that once He set them into motion, even God was bound by His Laws.*
>
> ⊙ ⊙ ⊙

So freedom places us in the bondage of our responsibility to God and Creation, but it is a responsibility devoutly to be wished. We are bound by the cords of freedom, but without them, we would be in bondage, unable to achieve anything higher.

Of Good and Evil

If only five to ten percent of us ever make full use of our freedom to become what God intended, what about the rest of humanity? They create evil. Now, that's not to say that all the rest are warring, whoring and murdering. Of course not. But they are creating miseries major and minor, discord in the harmony of God. Evil comes when we stop acting as God, when we forget that we are one with the Mind of God, and start acting as though our thoughts are nothing more than neural firings. Evil is the misuse of the Law of Freedom to do anything and everything instead of acting with vision and intention in mind.

How's this for a momentous idea? When the entire human race discovers its true self and everyone acts to bring about his or her tiny part in the great drama of God, evil will cease. That's right: evil will come to an end. No one will go hungry, no one will be killed in the streets for drug money, no one will cheat or steal from his neighbor. Those things only occur when people act out of accordance with their Divine nature. When we all learn that we were made to be the companions of the infinite, everything will change.

God merely waits for us to become aware of our true nature and to return His love.

☾ ☾ ☾

This answers the ancient question, "Why does God allow evil to exist in the world?" The answer is this: God does not allow anything. He created the Laws and us, and those opposing forces must play out according to their nature. Because we have freedom, we must be allowed to stray and return to the Father, to learn from our mistakes and come back to our true selves and to God. God merely waits for us to become aware of our true nature and to return His love. As he says in Revelations 3:20, "Behold, I stand at the door and knock." He is always knocking at the door of your true self. Sometimes, this freedom to stray becomes evil, death and destruction, because those are the choices that some people make. Evil is the willful misuse of the Law of Freedom. That is how it must be. God is not the answer to this dilemma; *we are.* We can only bring evil to an end by bringing awareness and enlightenment to all people of the nature of God's Laws and each man's duty to fulfill his destiny. As Holmes wrote, "Evil will disappear when we no longer indulge in it." Or as Julius Caesar put it in Shakespeare's play, "The fault, dear Brutus, lies not within our stars, but within ourselves."

An Absolute Force

All the Laws of Being are implacable, just as gravity is. They are blind forces unbound by any compassion or judgment. They simply respond to our actions in a way that matches their purpose. As there is no prejudice in gravitation, there is no prejudice in the misfortune that befalls a man who uses his freedom to betray his neighbor. It is what must happen.

There's a certain comfort in this. After all, we know that whatever we do will come back to us in kind, and that we have the freedom to do whatever we like. Therefore, we have the power to create any kind of effect or result in our lives. However, as with so many other facets of life, this is a double-edged sword. The Law of Freedom means we are living without a net; it can allow us to bring into our awareness anything and everything that we give our attention to, so we must be careful. There are no judges or juries to appeal to, no second chances. What is done cannot be undone. The law is utterly indifferent to human need or appeal.

Freedom from unhappiness comes from this knowledge, because we can see that we have total control over our lives. No one else is in the driver's seat! We don't have to be children and say to God, "You drive. I don't want to look." We don't have this luxury. We must take the wheel. But this also means no one else is dictating who or what we become today or tomorrow. We are really in control, and we can turn to God for instruction and vision. It's as if God is our instruction manual for putting His laws into action for our benefit...and His.

You will only come into Grace when you know the Law and its nature. It's impossible otherwise, because you are not operating as a mind within the Mind of God. As Florence Scovel Shinn writes, "The deliverance under Moses is the freedom gained from the taskmaster, as learned from the law of life, for we can never come under grace until we first know the law. The law must be made known in order to be fulfilled."

Choose Freedom

The Law of Freedom is no respecter of persons. It applies to everyone, regardless of station. There is no appeal that will blunt its effects to attract your acts you engage in into your existence. As Holmes says, it will be a law of freedom to those who engage in righteous acts and a law of bondage to those who choose to defy God's will. Your freedom to maneuver lies only in choosing to act from the right motive. In the right motive lies freedom.

What is the right motive? It is that which comes from your awareness of the Mind of God and your place as part of that Mind. When your actions are free of the tension that comes from opposing your God-ordained potential, then you are acting with right motive. When your choices are free from fear and filled with joy, laughter and lightness, you can be certain that you are acting in harmony with the designs of God and taking the right steps on your path as the regent of God's earthly design.

So when you fear your own decisions, heed the warning! You are very likely taking action that defies your Divine nature and will suffer the consequences. Your Divine nature, connected to the Mind of God, knows when your choices are counter to your true nature. The Law is the only law in our experience, the divine law we must obey. Listen to that still, small voice, otherwise known as your intuition. It will be a good guide to help you choose the path of Law.

Henry David Thoreau, who wrote *Walden,* chose freedom from the human jungle when he chose to build a small cabin in the woods and live in it for two years alone, contemplating nature and the self. You don't have to go to those extremes, but you do need to choose to follow the path of your freedom—to know the Law and reach the state of Grace that comes with embracing your place in God's work. As Thoreau wisely stated, "I know of no more encouraging fact than the unquestionable ability of a man to elevate his life by a conscious endeavor." Choosing freedom elevates your Spirit.

> *Choosing freedom elevates your Spirit.*
>
> ☾ ☾ ☾

Do the Unimaginable

Human society is a game of pretense. We are all pretending that we are acting selflessly, even though we are acting to help ourselves as well. You disagree? Ask yourself why you help the homeless or give to the poor. Because it is right, of course. But you also do so because it makes you feel good, or because you feel more holy when you choose such acts. Every action is self-serving in some way; there is nothing wrong with this, but it's important to understand.

When someone wants to help you, be certain you can also see where they are helping themselves. You must be vigilant for those whose intentions can carry your pursuit of freedom within God's purpose off course. You are not an island. Others can influence you, so you must be alert to the nature of their influence. You must be an island in terms of your commitment to God's freedom and your pursuit of the full realization of your nature within His plan.

See yourself as what you want to become...

With this awareness you are free to bring your impressions into being. Every impression is a feeling buried. It is your intuition speaking, your awareness of that tension between what you are doing and what God wishes of you. Pay attention, and infuse your subconscious with expectancy. See yourself as what you want to become; act as if you are already rich or accomplished and you can "fool" the material world into bringing that reality into being!

What unlocks the marvelous chemistry of this world is audacious action. Do the unimaginable, take risks, defy conventional wisdom, go against the grain. Grain represents the harvest, which is predictable. To go against the harvest is to strike out on an original path that others may disapprove of (in fact, it's a certainty that they will), but which can create new realities and incredible rewards. You have the freedom to do this. As Charles Fillmore writes, "There is a freedom in you to perform things that are unimaginable. God is free to do as He wills, and He has implanted that same freedom in man."

Awaken your imagination. Think as if there has never been any truth in your life but the realization of your dreams. Pay heed to your feelings and those desires that come to you unbidden, because they are from the mind that you share with God. God speaks to us in our unconscious mind and inspires our imaginations and creativity. Then turn that inner creator into inner speech and bring what you see in your mind's eye into being. Right speech is the key to becoming who and what your deepest passions tell you that you were *meant* to be. Listen to your passions, for they will speak loudly. That speech is a direct connection of your mind to the Mind of God.

Freedom is a state of consciousness. You are free to make the unimaginable imaginable, the extraordinary ordinary. That is God's purpose for you.

7

— THE LAW OF DIVINE GRACE —

ᘒ ᘒ ᘒ

Jesus wept, Voltaire smiled. From that divine tear and from that human smile is derived the grace of present civilization.

—Victor Hugo

In Second Corinthians 12:7, Jesus says, "My grace is sufficient for thee, for my power is made perfect in weakness." The matter of grace has been debated as long as there have been theologians. Who has grace? What is it? Can one earn grace or once one is out of God's grace, is one denied it forever? For centuries, strict Christian sects like the Puritans debated whether salvation could be earned by belief alone or whether good deeds were the key to grace. The question has stumped more than a few great theological minds.

Well, I'm here to tell you that we know the answer. It is "Neither." Neither belief in God and acceptance of Jesus Christ suffices, nor do good works do the trick. Those are both vitally important, but neither is enough to earn God's grace. Grace comes from one thing only:

LIVING, THINKING AND BEING COMPLETELY WITHIN GOD'S LAWS.

ᠣ ᠣ ᠣ

Grace, as you probably know from past studies, means "unmerited favor." That is, favor we do not deserve but which God lavishes upon as anyway as a merciful and loving parent. Well, that may be a good enough definition for some, but I disagree with it. That connotation of grace paints us as errant children and God as a disapproving parent bribed into giving us something we're unworthy of. That's an archaic and dogmatic view. Instead, we should call grace "earned favor," in that it is earned when we have the wisdom and maturity to set aside our short-sighted vision of life and embrace God's Laws in their fullest form. When we attune our consciousness to the fullness of God's economy and become that which we wish to accomplish, we earn God's grace. God desires us to become fully part of the Divine, to claim our inheritance.

Living and Set Free By the Word

In this state, the Word is all. The Word—awareness and full existence in and by the Laws of Being—is all the sustenance we need. This is why God's economy rewards risk takers, because they set aside all other means of support and rely 100% on the Laws for their bread, water and shelter. That is truly all you need! When Christ says His grace is sufficient for you, He means that it is the sole source you will need of plenty, wealth, health and joy. When you are living by the Word, your mind is fully in concert with the Mind of God and you are bringing your visions into manifestation out of the etheric plane. You should and do need nothing else.

There's true freedom in this, and in fact it's the nature of the Law of Freedom, which we just discussed. Divine Grace frees you from having to serve the masters of work, money, debt and other things and gives you the liberty to create your dreams. It also has a world-changing effect: you bring grace to others simply by being around them. When someone encounters your aura of grace, your vibration reaches into theirs and begins to bring it into synchrony with that Divine vibration. You can actually free others from karmic bondage by bringing grace into their awareness! This is why those who are operating in grace inspire others as leaders, CEOs, artists and so on. Every human cannot help but respond in some way to the aura of Divine Grace. Your higher self elevates others.

Being saved means becoming aware, a full participant in God's economy.

The beautiful thing is that this conversion to a state of Divine Grace can happen in the twinkling of an eye, at any time in your life. You have only to state "I Am" the blessing you desire to achieve, accept your place as God's co-creator and the custodian of part of His plan, and set aside all other paths you have been taking to get what you want. If you can live, mind and body, in the economy of Spirit, God's grace will rain upon you. That's all it takes. When we ask people to accept Jesus Christ as their Lord and Savior, we're actually misinforming them. We should be teaching them to accept Christ's teachings as the Master of God's System; that is the key to salvation in this life. We don't have to suffer and wait for a next life to realize Heaven, or Hell if that is what we choose. Being saved means becoming aware, a full participant in God's economy.

This change happens in the third eye of your understanding: your mind's eye, that intuitive perception that sees beyond the physical and perceives the Mind of God. As Joel Goldsmith writes, "In any moment, in the twinkling of an eye, a person can be reborn, but only because divine Grace has led him to that place, and if he is receptive to this message he, at any age that he finds himself, can come into the new consciousness."

The Power of "I Am"

That new consciousness ushers us into a new reality of Spirit. In this reality, one idea is all-powerful. Are you ready for the Idea that stands at the heart of the universe? The Concept that stood before Time and before the foundations of the earth were laid? This is the core Idea that God Himself relies upon to work His wonders. Are you ready for it? Are you ready to know that you can share in it in your role as a co-creator with God? Here it is:

ෆ ෆ ෆ

"I AM."

ෆ ෆ ෆ

That's it. Two words encompass immortality and eternity. Too simple, you say? Why? Why does the underpinning of the cosmos have to be complex or mysterious? Why can't it be elegant and simple? "I Am" is the sound of Divine Grace. It is the set of syllables that move galaxies and bring visions into material reality. "I Am" is life for us all, the way and the door to immortality. It is the basis of all mysticism.

But what does "I Am" mean? To state it clearly and unambiguously, "I Am" reflects the true nature of the cosmos, which is thought and consciousness. Many materialistic physicists and other scientists now cling to a dogma that says the universe is nothing more than a cold collection of elementary particles, gas and dust bound together by mindless physical laws. But as fringe researchers are beginning to discover, at its most basic level, the cosmos looks like a thought. It appears more and more likely that Consciousness is the First Cause of existence. With that being the case, intention becomes all-powerful. "I Am" is the nature of a universe in which thought has creative power, in which intention brings itself into material reality. In a nutshell:

☽ ☽ ☽

A CONSCIOUS MIND DECLARING THAT IT IS THE STUFF OF THAT WHICH IS DESIRED, AND THAT THE DESIRE IS ALREADY ACHIEVED, BRINGS THAT DESIRE INTO EXISTENCE.

☽ ☽ ☽

That conscious Mind is you, when you are functioning within God's Laws: aware of cause and effect, living in harmony and so on. When you want to make something manifest, you do not need to toil and sweat to create it. All you need to do is declare "I Am" that desire with all your mind and Spirit, and know and behave as if that desire has already been achieved. The cosmos brings like to like, plenty to plenty. When you have plenty in your mind, the cosmos will bring it to you in your material experience. That is the formula for Divine creation! When you reach that place, Divine Grace will be yours in abundance. It is waiting for you.

When He created the universe, God used precisely this. As pure Spirit, it was a natural to Him as breathing is for us. When He made the heavens, He didn't say, "I hope the heavens will show up." He declared that they already *were*. They became. This is a secret that our materialistic society has blinded us to, and it's a tragedy. Few can see clearly how wondrous this secret is and how beautifully simple it is to use. The difficult journey comes in bringing your Mind and Spirit to that place where you are part of the Mind of God and fully accepting that you must rely only on "I Am" to get what you want. That's not easy, especially for Americans, who still have our Puritan work ethic.

Preparing Your Consciousness

But if "I Am" is the destination, and you are on the road to that place, how do you walk the path to reach that state of being? To begin with, you must prepare your consciousness to receive Divine Grace. There is a simple way to do this: turn off your conscious, reasoning mind. Meditate or simply let your thoughts slide away and let yourself simply Be. You will find yourself going deep within to that place where feelings and intuition hold sway. This takes practice; we are quite accustomed to thinking and analyzing and doubting. It may take you some time to learn to quiet your mind, and certainly disciplines like yoga or mediation can help in this. Eventually, you will find your mind slipping into this relaxed, open state where you become like an antenna for the signals of the universe.

You must prepare your consciousness to receive Divine Grace.

It is this state that is most conducive to those extraordinary perceptions that most humans have forgotten how to use. The ability to sense and see into the minds of others, to look into the future, to see and sense what is distant—all these abilities known as "psi" are very real, but they are inhibited by our conscious minds, which filter out such signals so that we can focus on what appears to be the essential work of survival: working, toiling, making money. But when we set such supports aside and function only in God's economy and we can let our domineering conscious self slide away, we suddenly find new worlds of perception opening up.

That is the nature of grace: it is like a bank account always there for withdrawal. You have only to know the secret code of the ATM. And the amount that can be withdrawn is without limit; whatever demand you have in your life, whatever you desire to bring your vision into being or to deal with a difficult time, grace is always sufficient to meet it. When hard times come, it becomes more important than ever to turn to God's System and state your "I Am." Grace is boundless and will bring boundless solutions to you. God's grace is equal to any demand you can put upon it.

Secure In Your Interior World

Have you ever visited the Zen gardens of Buddhist monks, or the remote, walled monasteries of some of the Christian monastic orders? There is in these self-contained worlds an incredible peace and silence that washes over you, as a citizen of our loud, frantic world. It's almost like a blanket of tranquility that protects your mind from care. It is so easy to sit for hours without conscious thought, feeling utterly serene and at one with the universe. I venture to such spaces when I can to calm my Spirit.

Such spaces do not just exist in the exterior world. They exist within each of us, even if our physical environment is chaotic, rude and dangerous. You have an interior world where Divine Grace resides, and in that world you cannot be disturbed by the outer world. Once you have discovered the hidden gate into that secret garden within your Spirit, you will find you contain within you everything you need to create the outer world you envision. You need nothing else. The outer world can buffet and bump you, but it cannot touch your inner awareness or serenity.

That's why true holy people, men and women who live in a state of grace, appear so unflappable, so tranquil and joyous and unmoved by the harsh winds of the world. They know that within them is another universe subject to another set of laws. But when you achieve this state, it will not be obvious to anyone else. There can be no outer proof of inner perception; our science-minded culture does not recognize the reality of subjective experience. But subjectivity is the truth of existence, because only in our subjective minds do we come into contact with reality in Spirit.

> *...only in our subjective minds do we come into contact with reality in Spirit.*
>
> ☾ ☾ ☾

The experience of Noah is an example of this principle in action. Outside the Ark, all was chaos and death. Inside, where belief and faith ruled the day, everyone was safe from calamity. Inside your own ark of "I Am" and Divine Grace, you are protected from the calamity of the outside world.

Love X 7

Joel Goldsmith writes, "There is no other power than this divine Grace functioning within us, and Its mode of functioning is through love. Then we are permitting love, not our love, but God's love, to flow through us in the form of forgiving 'seventy times seven' in the form of praying for our enemies and for those who persecute us." Love is the force that powers God's Divine System, and we are compelled by it to show love to everyone in our sphere. That is your responsibility as you bring grace to others; that is the vibration we spoke of earlier. When other people encounter your unconditional love from a state of Divine Grace, they become "infected" with your love and their own hearts begin to transform. In this way, love changes the world.

In this universe, seven has a special significance. Think about how many ways the number appears in our experience. There are seven days in the week. There are seven notes in the musical scale. There are seven openings in the face: the eyes, ears, nostrils and mouth. There are seven bodies of man represented by the seven charkas. Seven is the number of perfection, and so when you forgive seven times 70 of the people in your life for their transgressions, you are engaging in a Divine act. Love is a kind of transmitter that carries grace to others, even if they do not share your level of consciousness. Every human being can feel that grace even if they are not attuned to it; our beings were made to respond to it.

In this same fashion, with Divine Grace you can know that you have all you need to live your life and reach the zenith of joy, prosperity and love without worrying about any other needs. Divine Grace rests within you at all times when you are in an "I Am" consciousness; it is never absent. That's incredibly freeing! You are absent concerns about money, position, power, even food and shelter. You always know that everything you need to sustain your life is within your Spirit, ready at a moment's notice to use thought to tape the creative energy of the universe. You can live in difficult times, in ill health or poverty, but not worry. You can accept the lessons that hard times bring while knowing that all the while the Divine Grace of God waits within you, and when the time is right and you have walked a certain path for a while, it will burst forth and bring you to great things. Divine Grace breeds Divine peace of mind.

Surrender and Find Power

What this amounts to is a state of Divine surrender. You can and must give over your will to Divine Grace and take no thought of the outward world. Such a thing is difficult for us with our overdeveloped egos. We see ourselves as prime movers in the universe, but we are wrong when we think of that power as stemming from our hands and our effort. Mind is everything. Our ability to grow and shape that world around us comes from setting aside the Self and fully existing in the light of Divine Grace. When we do this we can receive the wisdom that guides and shapes our actions outside of ourselves. Then we can move in the physical realm and we will quickly become very busy. There is more to do than ever before when we are motivated and guided by Spirit.

We can call this achieving *spiritual consciousness.* Spiritual consciousness is the state to which all enlightened individuals aspire, sort of a black belt in divinity. When you dwell in spiritual consciousness, you discover your spiritual power. You are elevated to the standing of creator, full participant in God's machinations to shape reality in flesh and Spirit. But it is vital to recognize this state for what it is. Spiritual consciousness is not power in the sense that we know it today; it is not the power to war with evil or the power to rule men. It is not the power to acquire wealth for its own sake. It is Divine Grace: it is the power to *be* and *become* that which God intended: your own unique source of light and enlightenment for others. Divine Grace is not power that you wield, but power that flows through you. It becomes part of your being, and others recognize it as Divine.

Divine Grace is not power that you wield, but power that flows through you.

ꙩ ꙩ ꙩ

To reach this sublime level of spiritual being, you must undergo a kind of death to your old way of being and experience a rebirth into a state of Divine Grace. Doing so, you follow the path of Christ, who died as a man only to be reborn as a higher being. Paul said, "I die daily," as he faced likely martyrdom for his spreading Christianity in the time after Christ's death. But what Paul meant was that he died each day to the world of men and was resurrected into the world of God's grace. You must do the same if you are to come into your inheritance. You must die to your old ways of pursuing a limited future and ignoring the power of your thoughts. You must let that way expire and instead turn away from it and live in your "I Am," becoming the change that you wish to see in the world.

As with anything as dramatic as death, the experience can be frightening. After all, you are letting go of the only mode of living you have ever known, the frame through which you regard the world. This is the leap of faith that so many speak of. Leaping from the material to the invisible, from the visible means of support to the unseen, interior world of "I Am" may appear insane to others. It may appear insane to you at first. But take the leap. That chasm is all that separates you from God's glory.

Going Into the Spiritual Realm

We're going to take a vacation, just the two of us. We're going to venture into the spiritual realm where anything is possible. But you need your passport. What is your passport to this world? Well, it should be clear by now. You must recognize and become your "I Am," that keystone thought in the Divine System. You have always held that passport within you, but you may never have recognized it until now. When you grasp that "I Am" in your consciousness, your thinking moves from its material base, your brain, to a spiritual base, your immortal Spirit. Your brain is limited in its scope and abilities, but your Spirit is one with God, who is Spirit, so you instantly expand your awareness and ability to shape reality infinitely.

This is what we have found the prophets doing throughout the Bible and for all of the existence of humankind. Men like Ezekiel and Jeremiah have shed their limited perceptions and preoccupations with the material realm and moved on in Spirit to the realm where Mind is the currency of power and transformation. They have taken their sustenance and clothing from the Divine Grace that is open to anyone who makes this journey; that is why they were able to walk among men often naked, with nothing but the power of their voices to sway others to give them food and drink so they might live. They knew that the Divine within even the most hardened of us responds instinctively to the Voice of grace.

The less we dilute Divine Grace with our own ego, the more freely will it pour into our experience and transform us and the world around us. When we are still and silent and turn off our conscious, argumentative minds, grace flows through us as through an open portal and changes our experience. It manifests as our desires, which we have held in our hearts but relied on God's economy to fulfill. That is how true blessings come. The prophets new of the drawing power of God to bring them what they needed. You must be as a modern-day prophet.

Your Law is Your Own

What a marvelous existence it must be to live at the same mental and spiritual pitch as the prophets, the first true servants of God. Because in this state of internal grace and functioning purely in Spirit, you step out of the laws of the world. You are not subject to the natural laws that plague men of lesser grace, because your continual "I Am" conscious-ness brings you what you need and shields you from the natural laws that govern most of our lives. You are less subject to the laws of weather and climate, because grace sends you warmth in Spirit and finds ways to keep your physical body comfortable and safe. You are less subject to the need for food because you receive spiritual nourishment. You are less subject to disease and health concerns, because Spirit keeps you healthy and prevents you from bringing illness into your experience through incorrect thinking. You even become less subject to the ravages of age and the calendar, as your true age is ageless, because Spirit is immortal. More and more you move into a life defined by Grace. Grace becomes your food and drink and air, bringing you everything you need.

This transformation is akin to the caterpillar turning into a butterfly. Imagine you are the caterpillar, a humble material creature consumed with the need to eat and eat. One day, you find the urge to spin a chrysalis out of silk, and into this chamber you retreat to undergo a miraculous metamorphosis. The moment you relinquish your faith in the material world and see Spirit and Divine Grace as your sole sources of comfort and plenty, you crawl into your own chrysalis. When you dwell fully in your "I Am" state and receive Divine Grace in its fullness, you emerge as the caterpillar, changed into a butterfly.

This is your transition—the transition all people who bear God's enlightenment must pursue. You are consciousness in transition, taking the Mind that is your infinitely small share of the Mind of God and turning it into your reality. Consciousness is everything. You move, as Joel Goldsmith writes, from sitting at the feet of the Master to sitting at the table of the Master. You realize your own puissance as a co-Creator. As Goldsmith writes, "I have received from the Master. From Truth I have received life eternal. I have received divine Grace. I

Consciousness is everything.

෧ ෧ ෧

have received the assurance of my Oneness with God. Now it is my turn to share, to bless, and to pray."

Master Your Destiny

So yes, much is asked of you. But much is given: the freedom to choose, the awareness of Spirit simmering right beneath your conscious mind, the power to transform your experience and physical world by embracing "I Am" as your means of existence. By becoming that which God intended, by living according to Divine Grace, you in a sense are repaying God for the potential to become what you become. Your fulfillment of your potential is also the fulfillment of God's plan. When you reach the state where nothing of this world is of importance to you, you will begin to walk that path of Divine Mastery, a state in which nothing is impossible. You become one with God's Mind and you shed all need for the shallow trappings of the material plane.

The God within you, that is part of the infinite Father, is equal to any demand.

Yes, you must continue to live in the material world. Your body will continue to need food and water, you will continue to need clothing and so forth. But those things will not dominate your consciousness. You will see yourself finally as you truly are: an agent of the Almighty sent to this reality to carry one spark in the roaring flame of His Divine plan for the cosmos. Your Divine consciousness will bring forth action of its own accord, shaping the world according to God's Will. There is no need or obligation that Divine Grace cannot meet, no emptiness it cannot fill forever. The God within you, that is part of the infinite Father, is equal to any demand. Your burdens are God's burdens, and in Spirit they are lifted.

To bring this greatness into your life, you must take control of your destiny. As Ernest Holmes said, "I am the captain of my ship." None but you can choose to transform and embrace your destiny in Spirit. However, when you finally do this, you will discover an interconnectedness that opens your eyes to the true nature of reality. Nothing is separate. We are all connected through Divine Grace to God and each other. Divine Grace touches the consciousness of everyone who perceives it. Just imagine that day when all humanity is united in grace and we all share the sense of oneness and universal love that is our birthright! We will become what we have always been, and what illusion has prevented us from seeing: one family.

8

— THE LAW OF SUPPLY AND DEMAND —

⊖ ⊖ ⊖

As scarce as truth is, the supply has always been in excess of the demand.

—Josh Billings

In his letter to the Philippians, Paul of Tarsus wrote, "And my God shall supply every need of yours according to his riches in glory in Christ Jesus." God shall supply. The reality of supply and demand is as old as Creation. But as we shall see, it is not applied equally. The Law of Supply and Demand is a law of limitation—where demand exceeds supply, there is want. Where supply exceeds demand, there is stagnation. According to this law, you are limited in what you can have. Yet that is precisely why we must expand beyond ourselves and live according to a spiritual path, as did the prodigal son. Only then are we freed from the limitations of supply and demand.

We learn the formula of supply and demand in our high school economics classes. When supply outstrips demand, prices drop. When demand overtakes supply, prices rise. But this is a Law based on the material world, and our discussions in the past few chapters have been about transcending the material and living as pure consciousness. Let me share with you that consciousness is freedom from the want of supply and demand! There can be no such thing as need when you are consciousness, because you wield the power to turn your thoughts into things. You cannot know want because you *are* plenty. Reality is either one of Spirit and consciousness of "I Am", or it is the worry about life's necessities that comes with being bound to supply and demand. When you exist primarily as a being of consciousness, your individual consciousness *becomes* your supply. That supply, whatever you desire, will sprout inevitably from your thought as grain must sprout from a seed dropped in the earth and watered by the rain.

The Nature of Desire

Within the bounds of conventional Christianity, there is a deep misunderstanding and mistrust of earthly desire. Francis of Assisi spent his life trying to shed his desire for earthly pleasures. But does God really see desire as sinful? This is yet another misunderstanding of the reality of the material world and how it relates to the spiritual, a holdover from the self-imposed shame of our Puritan ancestors. They assumed that all material pleasure was a distraction from the constant adoration of God, so they shunned it. But as we know today, this was mistaken.

> *God does not despise desire.*
>
> ༄ ༄ ༄

God does not despise desire. Quite the opposite. In fact, when you exist in God consciousness as a creature of Spirit, your desires are quite naturally sent by God to indicate to you that something is waiting for you in the endless realm of supply that waits for your declared thought to make it reality. That's right: God sends you desires because he wants you to know what is possible—what is meant for you to have. As Jack Ensign Addington writes, "Desire in the heart is God tapping at the door of consciousness with His infinite supply. If the desire is there, then it is certainly possible to achieve it."

To bring this promised supply into material experience, you have but to declare "I Am" that which you desire. This stems from God's speech to Moses on Mount Sinai, when the Lord told Moses, "I Am that I Am." The Laws set down by God confer ultimate potency on the spirit-centered declaration of what *is,* not the hopeful statement of what will be. When you desire success, you will state, "I Am success." When you wish health, you will declare, "I Am health." When you need strength to see you through life's hard times, you will tell the cosmos, "I Am strength." And through that fearless statement of being, your thoughts will draw that reality from the ether into your reality.

Supply is a State of Mind

In metaphysics, supply and demand are the same thing. Supply is a state of mind, but it does not exist without demand. Demand is the opportunity or occasion to bring supply into existence to fill a need. Let's say that you have the desire to open a business in your neighborhood. Your desire is a manifestation of what God means for you to have in your experience, so you declare the reality of that desire and watch it come into being over a period of a few months. When it does, you find that you are able to hire other people from your neighborhood, people who had recently lost their jobs. So

> *Supply is a state of mind, but it does not exist without demand.*
>
> ○ ○ ○

unknown to you, your supply was sparked by the demand for employment—the need of others to have work, earn a living and retain their pride. Supply drives demand, but demand also drives supply.

Whenever you are ready to experience something, you will find that supply is ready to come to you. There is no wrong time for anything when you dwell in Divine Grace and God consciousness; every desire manifests when it should, not a moment before or after. Your job is to listen to that voice of desire welling up inside you and put God's Laws to work making it material reality. That is the role each of us has been ordained by the Lord to play, each of us weaving one tiny strand in the infinite web of life and evolving Spirit.

> *We must follow the Laws consciously, which requires much discipline and wisdom.*
>
> ♫ ♫ ♫

"In such a state of consciousness, we are no longer under the law of supply and demand; we are no longer under the law of economics; we are no longer under the law of the amount of our supply of gold, silver, or currency. We have brought ourselves out from under the law and placed ourselves under Grace, but this must be done as a specific act of our own consciousness." So writes Joel Goldsmith in *Living by the Word,* and his point is well taken. Rather than conform to the normal laws of supply and demand, we must transform ourselves and our awareness to the pitch of the Laws of Being. We must follow the Laws consciously, which requires much discipline and wisdom. But when we can reach this elevation of grace and consciousness, we become our own laws of need and plenty. We no longer live from a place of want. We *become* our own bounty.

The Mental Science

There is no gap between supply and demand. The demand that calls upon you to exercise your elevated consciousness leads to supply as seamlessly as clouds lead to rain; it cannot be otherwise. Supply and demand are two sides of the same coin.

Supply always follows demand in exactly the proportions that are needed to meet the demand. There is never any lack. The widow woman of Zarephath, to whom Elijah was sent for food and shelter, did not grasp this reality. She spoke from a place of want only, saying that she had just enough meal and oil to make one cake for herself and her son, then they would lay down and die of hunger. This never occurred, of course, because of God's grace. But the woman would have saved herself much anguish if she had understood that she was already the fount of all she needed.

> *Supply and demand are two sides of the same coin.*
>
> ○ ○ ○

This is the mental science of demand. It takes us back to the Law of Compensation, by which every word or action breeds a response from the universe that is its like. As you develop in God consciousness, you must and will learn to govern and control your mind and what your thoughts breed out of demand. Imagine the chaos and misfortune that would result if every idle thought and desire became reality! We simply can't have such a thing, so spiritual masters learn to cosset their minds and only think in ways that exalt man and serve God. If you lose control of your consciousness, there's no way of knowing what the implacable Laws will deliver into your world: misfortune, disease, betrayal.

Can you achieve this level of mental and spiritual mastery? Just as with the great martial artists, the raw potential exists within us all.

However, potential without discipline and guidance is like a karate black belt kicking at a sheet of paper: the paper does not conform to his rules, so he can do nothing. If you don't discipline your mind and actively build the consciousness you seek, you will find yourself a victim of the Law of Unintended Consequences. You are on this material plane in order to comprehend and master the Laws of Being.

The Matter of Money

You are also here to understand the nature of money. Money is so often the focus of our lives, but it rarely is supplied in sufficient volume to buy us the things we think we need to make a difference. But that is an illusion. Money is the power of change made manifest, but it is also the symbol of your comprehension and your life's journey. You must understand money if you are going to make this trek into the deep country of God's economy. Project your energies into money-making activities but do not worry about them actually generating money right away. Merely fill them with the thought and intent of money, and wealth will flow your way. Once you can project your Divine energy into your moneymaking activities, you will discover that demand is no longer an isolated activity. Instead, it propels supply and makes things possible in your experience.

You are also here to understand the nature of money.

Projection of your spiritual energy into moneymaking ideas is the secret to wealth. It is why you see so many of the wealthiest people like Donald Trump constantly moving at high speeds from one project to the next. They don't longer over the details and micromanage; they imbue their ideas with their wealth-centered consciousness then move on, leaving the people in their employment to handle the details and bring their ideas to fruition. They are like farmers sowing seeds of money. Once you become a purveyor of ideas and trust the spiritual energy of God's Laws to bring those ideas into being, you will enjoy material and spiritual wealth beyond the limits of supply and demand.

The other secret to wealth? Give people what they want, not what they need. Imagine a benefactor who helped you become more prosperous in your own right. You would give that person a tithe of your new riches in thanks, wouldn't you? Of course. But when some entrepreneurs look to build their businesses, they approach things from a position of *want*. They look to fill the *needs* of others, ignoring the truth that there is always an oversupply of demand. But as we've seen, the universe rewards like with like, so if you focus on the lack of something, you will get back that same lack. You don't give people what they need. You give them what they want.

But as we've seen, the universe rewards like with like...

♪ ♪ ♪

Calvary was a suicide mission because Christ was giving the people what they needed, a scapegoat for the political leaders of the time. There was no other outcome possible, and He knew this. He accepted it. But we are not fomenting political or religious change; we're just trying to transform our corner of the world for the better! So forget about what people need. Let them have their own drama. Focus on that which people don't even know they want, something that elevates them, or as Stuart Wilde writes, "If you can't give people one thing imbued with an energy that shines like crazy, you can find something else they'll want." When you can do this, the people whose eyes and hearts you open will make you rich beyond words.

Market? What Market?

Millions of people around the country live and die by the fluctuations of the stock market. They watch its gyrations like a family member watching an intensive care patient's vital signs. They base their fortunes on its rise and fall. But this is a kind of bondage, a dependency on man's markets and man's supply. It limits what you can do and who you can become, links you to the fates and decisions of millions of others who may not be capable of making the same kinds of wise decisions that you make. The solution should be obvious: do not conform to man's markets!

The solution should be obvious: do not conform to man's markets!

ᘐ ᘐ ᘐ

When the God consciousness is at the center of your being, you are your own market, your own economy. You are capable of tapping the infinite flow of riches and creative energy that fills the cosmos, so you are outside of the ordinary laws of supply and demand. You are exempt from the laws. This can confound the other people in your life who do not yet know the truth. Even when times are lean for others, your hands will flow with wealth and opportunity, and they will wonder, "How?" How can you possibly defy the material markets that are the obsession of billions? You don't defy them; you bypass them completely. And as your aura and vibration reach out to others, you will bring them into harmony with your Spirit-centric self and slowly they, too, will undergo the same transformation.

Imagine a company made up of people who work in God consciousness. Imagine an organization whose central business tenet is "Supply and demand are one and there is no lack or want." Such an organization would be a powerhouse of wealth creation and world-changing power for good. It would be miles and miles beyond the competition and anyone else on earth. It would not matter if others did not agree with its ideas or approach; pioneers are frequently scorned and warned that they are headed down the road to ruin. But as Holmes writes, "We cannot demonstrate beyond our ability to mentally embody an idea. The argument is between our experience, what the world believes, and what we are convinced is the Truth."

> *Imagine a company made up of people who work in God consciousness.*
>
> ❍ ❍ ❍

This fact is the reason that no company, no matter how successful, should ever go public and sell shares on the stock market. Companies do it all the time and generate vast wealth for their shareholders. But in doing so, what do they do? They subject themselves to the demands of the material markets and the limited thinking of millions of brokers, buyers, analysts and reporters. Instead of being driven by the passion, vision and pure God-given creative energies of their founders, they become driven by small-minded market forces. They fail in their mission to spread the truth about God's laws. Often they fall into corruption and greed, as with Enron. Any enterprise that depends on man's markets, not God's infinite supply, is doomed to meanness, limit and want.

Your Want Detox

"The Lord is my shepherd; I shall not want." So says the 23rd Psalm, and it contains much wisdom. With God's economic secret in your consciousness, want is a thing of the past. However, you will not reach that state of infinite supply as long as want dominates your thinking. Remember the Law of Compensation? The universe gives like in response to like, so when you approach life from a direction of "I wish I had this," then the universe will bring that sense of lack and longing right back to you. You will not receive the things you desire without sweat and toil. But life doesn't have to be that way.

You must move, as Emmet Fox says, from longing to the statement and belief that you already have what you desire. In a way, you must fool the infinite supply of the universe into believing that you already possess plenty so it should reward you with more. This is possible because thought is the currency of the cosmos and shapes all its ends. When you train your mind not just to think but to exist in a mindset of plenty and shed any and all thoughts of want, you will attract plenty and endless supply to you. This is the real Law of Attraction!

Making this happen means undergoing a "detoxification" from want. We have been trained by our modern, materialistic culture to want what we want, to focus on our material needs and express to others our dissatisfaction at what we do not have. We say, "I wish I had a car like that," or "I hope we can save enough money to buy that house." But that language races into the ether and shapes what we receive. When we broadcast want, we receive want and lack of supply in return! It is the law of the cosmos. Detoxing from want means changing how you speak, think and live. You must begin living *as if the things you desire are already in your possession.* In fact, you must become those things! You are the grand house, you are the fine automobile, you are the full bank account.

> *You are money and prosperity.*
>
> ☾ ☾ ☾

You are money and prosperity. God's economy will respond in kind and manifest more of your reality in your experience. That is how the spiritual economy works!

How does one detox from the pervasive culture of "want" that we have created? Here are some suggestions:

- Consciously eliminate the word "want" from your vocabulary. Come up with an alternative.

- Create a verbal affirmation about the desires you wish to manifest in your life and speak them at least 3 times a day as if they have already come to pass. "I roam the rooms of my beautiful mansion each morning and enjoy the beauty out my windows," would be one example. Train your mind to think of these desires as achieved.

- Thank God throughout the day for bringing you what you have already received in your mind.

- When you run up against lack (not having enough money to buy a new pair of pants, for example), immediately close off thoughts like, "I wish I had..." and instead look at the ways that your demand might already be met by supply in your life.

Detoxing from the impulse to want takes time, but you can do it, and it will yield incredibly things for you.

Supply is Waiting for Your Demand

The hunger within you that you might interpret as want is actually the Divine prompting you to spend your consciousness capital to manifest supply. Supply is waiting for your demand at all times and in limitless quantities, because in the Spirit economy of God there is no lack. Supply wants to respond to demand; they are paired and must work together, catalyzing change and wealth and good for you and others. When you feel yourself building with passion for an outcome, an object or a goal, that is Divine desire telling you it's time to get busy and start working your "I Am" to bring forth the riches that await you. As we read in Mark 11:24, "Whatever you ask for in prayer, believe that you have received it and it shall be yours." If you ask from your God consciousness, the cosmos will always answer with supply. It has no choice: it must follow the Laws.

In reality, demand and supply are one. They are signal and prompting and fulfillment and potential realized. There is no difference in the end between the demand that inhabits your mind and manifests itself in your Divine thinking and the supply that comes forth from the stream of time, already created in Spirit, to become visible and tangible in our reality. They are both part of the same equation of spiritual physics: God implants desire in order to compel you to bring forth supply that evolves demand to a higher state. In this way, want gives way to wiser demand, and over time demand and desire become holy vision that shapes the world according to God's designs.

You must always ask from a place of faith if you are to receive supply.

Asking, then, becomes a matter of faith. You must always ask from a place of faith if you are to receive supply. Every time you send out a thought of pure faith from the "I Am" part of your mind, you set in motion an irresistible cascade of forces that will bring you the supply you seek. This is the debit card that unlocks the accounts of the invisible and eternal, as Charles Fillmore writes: "Ask whatsoever you will in the name of the Christ, the I AM, the divine within, and your demands will be fulfilled; both heaven and earth will hasten to do your bidding."

Strive for Better

You cannot and will not want for anything once you understand the true nature of God and the Law of Supply and Demand: that in Divine consciousness, supply and demand are one. When you internalize this reality, you will always strive for better and better results in your life. If better supply is available, good is not good enough. To bring about God's design, you should always be looking to achieve the best better result, to become greater and wealthier and more of a benefactor. That is the intent of God: for you to expand in wisdom and "prosperity consciousness" and continually improve your place in the world and that of others. In this way the material plane evolves toward the spiritual.

There is an invisible mental door of supply, a passageway to the endless warehouses of God's economy. If you're not finding the door, try doing something different. Try training your mind, thinking about your desires as already achieved, or simply seeing what you want as already existing in your mind's eye. You will be astonished at how riches and opportunity flow your way, great people come into your life from nowhere, and illness and misfortune will fade from your experience like the morning dew under the light of the sun.

You see, in prosperity consciousness, poverty becomes impossible. It is your responsibility as one of God's regents on this planet to bring that consciousness, and the freedom from the tyranny of markets that it brings, to as many of your fellows as possible. When we have done this, we will go a great distance toward eradicating poverty from the earthly realm. When all God's children have a place at the table, that will truly be the beginning of Heaven in the material world.

9

— THE LAW OF ACTION AND REACTION —

༡ ༡ ༡

The excessive increase of anything *causes a reaction in the* opposite direction.

—*Plato*

We have already discussed the Law of Cause and Effect, so what, you might ask, makes the Law of Action and Reaction different? That's a good question, and I will answer it here. The difference between the two laws is that while Cause and Effect govern all forces in the universe, conscious and unconscious, Action and Reaction apply only to deliberate action. So while Cause and Effect determines both the movement of the tides and the result of anger, Action and Reaction works only in the realm of the choices we make and their consequences. So let us look at that dynamic and see how it fits into the God consciousness we have begun to develop.

In Galatians 6:7, Scripture says, "Be not deceived; God is not mocked: for whatsoever a man soweth, that shall he also reap." That cannot be any clearer, and it defines the relationship our choices and actions have to our outcomes and destiny. While, as Ernest Holmes writes, we have a pattern of perfection woven into our very nature when we abide by God's Laws, we must discover that pattern through right choice and action. Thought that brings great things into being is considered action. Approaching the world from a position of want and desperate need is a considered action. If we are to discover the pattern of perfection that resides in our cells, organs and mind, we must make wise choices that lead to fruitful actions using God's economy as the source of all.

Thought that brings great things into being is considered action.

୨ ୨ ୨

This truly requires adjusting our psychology, training our mind to approach the challenges of this life from a Spirit-centric point of view, rather than a material need point of view. We must align our psychology with God's theology if we are to make full use of His System and bring total prosperity into our lives.

Singing in Harmony

We spoke of the Law of Harmony. The Law of Action and Reaction calls on us to see the harmony in the Divine whole—to see that in God's System, nothing is truly opposed, even if it appears to be so in the material world. Every aspect of you and your life—your body, your mind, your friends, your food, your job, your money—is in harmony with the purpose and will of God. There is nothing you cannot ask for that will not be given.

However, it takes some doing to get to that state of being. The Law of Action and Reaction within us knows everything that we do and the material and spiritual planes respond in kind to our every action and thought. Writes Joel Goldsmith, "Every thought we think and every act we perform, set in motion a law of action and reaction. If we sow to the flesh, we reap corruption. The law within us knows what we are doing, and it rewards us accordingly." So reaching that place where you are in complete harmony with the purpose and System of God requires tuning your entire being, especially your mind, to the pitch of God consciousness. We already know how to do this. Proverbs 20: 27 tells us, The spirit of man is the lamp of the Lord, searching all the innermost parts of his being." We have an innate knowledge of God down to the cellular level.

Becoming one with our Divine purpose takes work and time, but it can be done at any age. It is never too late to discover your spiritual legacy.

Think As You Would Experience

The Divinity of man is a truth, not a doctrine. We partake of the wholeness and vision of God through both the human ministry and Divine nature of Christ. That nature within us means that our thoughts have causal power just as God's thoughts are the creative power of the universe. So if we wish to experience the world in a certain way, we must think that experience into existence. Every one of our thoughts projects into the cosmos with the might of intentionality behind it

> *Your life is a self-fulfilling prophecy.*
>
> ୨ ୨ ୨

and sets events and energies in motion. This is the essential nature of existence with Consciousness as its fulcrum! Your reality is a thought, and the material world around you the result of your past thinking. Your life is a self-fulfilling prophecy. Eric Butterworth phrases it like this: "Do as you would be done by, think as you would like to experience, love and you shall be loved, forgive and you shall be forgiven. Jesus did not announce this as a new law. He did not create laws; He simply discovered them as part of the Divinity of Man."

This means that to have the plenty and endless supply we've been speaking of, you have to *discipline your mind.* There are consequences for every choice and every action; everything you do sets reactions in motion, many of which you cannot perceive. In many cases, you will not see these reactions at all, because they are so subtle. But you cannot see the food you eat reacting with your cells to create energy, yet your food powers your physical form. There are always consequences.

Your thoughts are the price you pay for what you wish to receive. There can be nothing received without payment; that is the vital balance that maintains the cosmos in its structure. Without that balance, effect would follow cause and there would be chaos. If you desire something with all your heart but fail to pay for it with the right "I Am" thinking that works within God's economy, then you will always receive something, but it will not be what you intended or desired. The Law always works, but it does not have to work for your benefit. You decide what its final effect will be based on the price you pay. The phrase "pay attention" is not an accident, but a reflection of the true economy of Spirit. You must pay the right kind of attention to the universe in order for God's Laws to deliver the result you crave.

> *You decide what its final effect will be based on the price you pay.*

The Completeness of Being

It is not in our nature to act with just part of our being and let the rest lie fallow. Within each of us is a crucial harmony of all aspects—dark and light, mind and Spirit, need and fulfillment. We are meant to use all aspects at all times. That is the only way in which we can spend the spiritual capital of our right thoughts. We are designed to operate in wholeness, including in our perception of action and reaction. The two cannot be separated, as one inevitably leads to another. So when you act without heed of what the reaction will be, your results will be disjointed, negative and even destructive. Think of a hungry man who robs another to get a single bite of food; is he acting with the reaction in mind? No, he is thinking only of his need, but he will end up in jail where his Spirit will suffer even more greatly. That is the reaction to action without foresight.

When we act with all our mind and heart in concert, the end is different. Everything we do is done with everything we have, and love, compassion, justice and knowledge shine through the result. We cannot turn a false face to others while harboring envy or rage inside. We reflect the completeness within us. Who we are outside is whole and in synch with our inner self. In understanding this, we will never again pressure or manipulate another. Why, when we would only end up putting pressure on ourselves? When we understand the unity of action and reaction, we become far more aware of the implications of each step we take. Mindfulness becomes not just a habit but the core of our existence.

Gratitude in Your Attitude

Minister Henry Ward Beecher said, "Gratitude is the fairest blossom which springs from the soul." He had an insight into the nature of gratitude that relates to the truth of Action and Reaction. Gratitude is almost a law unto itself, it has such power. Remember that in the Laws, like always reacts to like and what is sown shall be reaped. So the effect of grateful thought is to bring forth thanks from the cosmos. Action and reaction work in equal and opposite directions. This is why it is so wise to praise and thank God for your blessings: not because it is flattery, but because it looses the power of His economy and liberates creative energy. When you show gratitude in your every moment and thought, God will instantly respond by sending good in your direction.

So you must have gratitude in your attitude, always! Doing so creates an equal and opposite reaction. You should also express gratitude toward everything and everyone. The reason is simple: God is everywhere and everything. Every particle of matter and every mind in the human beings you pass on the street partakes of the wholeness that is God. Remember, each person is a being created to fulfill a microscopic but vital aspect of the Divine design; that deserves your respect. So be grateful to everyone and everything. The reaction will be swift and unavoidable, as the conditions of the Law require it to transform the conditions of your experience. Praise God and thank Him for what you have, and praise and thank other people and the material world around you, and you transform it all.

> *You should also express gratitude toward everything and everyone.*
>
> ☉ ☉ ☉

Some may see this as a source of trepidation. So you're telling me that when I get angry at a parking meter, I'm setting myself up for a ticket later on? In some cases, yes. But don't just look at the negative side of the equation. That's like looking at sunshine and thinking only how it can give you a sunburn. It's all in the choices you make! You *choose* to show anger or gratitude to that which is in your life. The results are automatic. Garbage in, garbage out. You will get what you put into the etheric economy. It is mindless and implacable. Even God must obey His Laws. Action and reaction are as automatic as gravity pulling on a baseball when it is hit. It will always fall back to earth. Your thoughts and actions will always fall back into your life.

Nothing Personal

Holmes writes, "Now science observes how these principles work. It studies the action and reaction of thought and emotion in the human mind; but it doesn't know what the human mind is. It studies the actions and reactions of life in the body; but it does not know what life is." Very true. Science has no explanation for the nature of consciousness and has trouble even acknowledging that it plays a causal role in reality, preferring to dismiss it as random neural firings. But the truth remains that whether we understand these things or not, they continue to function. Even if we did not understand the sun, it would continue to shine.

...whether we understand these things or not, they continue to function.

So the delivery of the results of our actions into our lives, both good and bad, is not a personal result of some decision of God, but the unavoidable result of the Laws He has set down. In a very real sense, the only way in which action and reaction are personal is when the intent comes from ourselves. When the subconscious mind, which science is discovering to be amazingly active and powerful, chooses to compel us to sabotage ourselves with a thought or deed, then the result could be said to be personal. But we have chosen to bring evil into our material reality; God had nothing to do with it. There is an aspect of "you get what you deserve" to this, but that is not how I choose to phrase it. I think it is rather, "you get what you pay for."

Here's another conundrum for conventional science, which has its own heresies and orthodoxies: there is nothing but Consciousness. As we are beginning to see in the quantum world, Consciousness is the fundament of the cosmos and all existence. In fact, all reality is the action and reaction of the universe, the cosmic Intelligence carrying out its mathematically precise responses to all thought. This is a philosophical position called *computationalism*, which argues that the entire cosmos is a vast mathematical equation playing itself out in the computer of planets and galaxies, cells and humans. While that may seem impersonal (and it is in a way), it really reflects the true nature of the Programmer of that computer, God. God is not an intervening God but a lawgiver. He is God as Mathematician, laying down the vital equations that will carry out His vision for His creation. There is intent behind everything, even if its operation can seem unconscious.

> *There is intent behind everything, even if its operation can seem unconscious.*
>
> ༄ ༄ ༄

Principles of Mind

Let's talk about the principles of Mind, the Mind that lies at the heart of all existence. It has its laws and rules, and following them will make your own thoughts more productive. First of all, there's prayer. Your prayers are more effective when you believe in the Law of Action and

Reaction, because what comes back to you does so in direct proportion to your belief. But God will not break His own Laws to answer your prayer; even prayer has limitations. This is why all the prayers to bring back a dead loved one have never worked; the death was a fair consequence of an action such as disease or violence, so it must stand according to the Laws.

God Himself is a principle of Mind, and He requires the action of His creation, us, to reach full fruition. Remember that God created us in order that He might influence the material plane. God is pure Spirit, so He cannot act directly in the corporeal world. He must work with his Creation to leverage His Laws to bring about the actions and reactions that shape the material cosmos in accordance with his design. When I said that you were a co-creator with the Lord, I was serious. We each have a vital role to play in bringing God's vision to life. We are all bit actors in a vast drama, each small but indispensable. As Holmes wrote, "When we think and work in unity with the Father, the results are universally good."

We are all bit actors in a vast drama, each small but indispensable.

ↄ ↄ ↄ

Another principle of Mind is that thought is circular. The truth of Consciousness as the substrate of all reality is reflected in this, as the great physicists found when they discovered that subatomic particles and great planets all move in circular patterns. The cycle is part of the natural world in the seasons, the cycle of birth and death, the cycle of sowing and reaping and so on. The same is true in the spiritual world, as we see with the circular motion of action and reaction. When you initiate an action or thought, it flies into the spiritual realm but eventually the reaction circles back to you, its source.

You will not be able to function well in this reality until you understand this pattern. This is the source of the idea of karma, or "what goes around comes around." In this reality, your actions lead to reactions that are in proportion to what you have set in motion. Good breeds good, ill breeds ill. As we said earlier, you are not punished for your sins, but by them. Comprehension of this canonical truth is key if you are to experience plenty and avoid misfortune and illness.

Shaping the Flow of Time

"History is the action and reaction of these two, Nature and Thought, two boys pushing each other on the curbstone of the pavement. Everything is pusher or pushed: and matter and mind are in perpetual tilt and balance, so. Whilst the man is weak, the earth takes up him." So wrote Ralph Waldo Emerson in talking about the power that the give and take of action and reaction have to shape how time plays out in this cosmos. No action is isolated; all things spark further actions and those their reactions. The result is a dizzyingly complex web of interlocking acts and responses, like a trillion billiard balls all careening off each other. This is causality, the force of Mind setting material in motion. The balance between Nature and Thought—also seen as the unconscious and the conscious—is the elemental ground state of reality.

That reality works, which is why it exists. Everything began with original Intelligence, and in a way all that has occurred since the Beginning has been in part the reaction to that initial creative Action. Holmes expressed it beautifully when he wrote, "There is only What Is and the way It works. There can be nothing in the Universe ultimately but action and reaction, the action being conscious intelligence and awareness, and the reaction intelligence unconsciously operating without awareness." When you look at reality from this perspective, action and reaction are the same thing. All actions are also reactions to some other action, which were in turn reactions to something else. The two are eternally linked and intertwined, thus the complex nature of reality that can only be deciphered by God.

So if you don't like the result of something in your life, what are you to do? Why, change your action, of course. But what if your action was the reaction to something else? Oh dear, this is getting complicated. The answer is not to change either your action or reaction but your *mind*. Change how you react to events and how your thoughts flow in response to the things that happen to you. Stop (as much as you can) the billiard balls and become an initiator of action, not a reactor. If you can do this, your action and the thought that begins it can have a purer reaction. You will have more control over what comes into your experience.

Science and Rules

Finally, look at ancient natural science. The purveyors like Democritus and Archimedes perceived patterns of systems in everything. They saw that all things reacted to each other in a web of natural laws. There was no Mind behind the reactions, yet still the laws operated. Through specific actions and reactions and causes and effects, results were produced. Understanding this led the ancients to escape the victim mentality of past ages—the idea that man was simply buffeted by godlike forces over which he had no control. Instead, we have learned that the universe is one of order and predictability.

Astrology came from this thinking, the idea that the patterns in the heavens determine and reveal human destiny. Modern science has rejected this idea, but there are still those who practice astrology as a serious art, not a parlor game, who can use it to predict much of the movements and fates of men.

Learning these truths, the patterns in the systems that surround us, is the vital skill that you must learn if you are to make full use of the Laws to manifest what you wish. God wants us to gain knowledge, to be sublime in our thinking. In Psalms 90:12, Scripture reads, "Teach us to number each of our days so that we may grow in wisdom." That means we must be fully aware of not only the passage of time but of each of the actions and thoughts we take during those days, so that we can evolve into God consciousness and become fully in control of the reactions that the Laws send us. To be full co-creators with God, we must attain that sort of wisdom. It can take a lifetime.

> *Action is reaction. When you incite, you invite.*
>
> ⊙ ⊙ ⊙

But the effort is not without reward. God is a rewarder, for good or ill. He will bring to you riches based on your wisdom. If you practice prosperous thinking, prosperity will appear in your corporeal existence. The Golden Rule of Prosperity is this: don't think or say anything about anyone else's finances that you do not want to happen to yours. Action is reaction. When you incite, you invite. Wish prosperity for all, and watch the rising tide of the Laws lift your boat as well as others.

10

— THE LAW OF PATTERNED THOUGHT —

ᗺ ᗺ ᗺ

Self-discipline, although difficult, and not always easy while *combating negative emotions, should be a defensive measure. At least we will be able to prevent the advent of negative conduct dominated by negative emotion. That is 'shila', or moral ethics. Once we develop this by familiarizing ourselves with it, along with mindfulness and conscientiousness, eventually that pattern and way of life will become a part of our own life.*

—*The Dalai Lama*

Everything has a pattern, as we are learning. Often that pattern is circular, but even if the pattern adopts a different shape it will still manifest consistently in every area of life. Behavior is the most patterned of all things for a reason: God designed it so. The Law of Patterned Thought dictates that your mind will always work in patterns; there is no escaping that. What you do have control over is what those patterns will be. The nature of your patterns of thinking will determine your reality.

Sadly, many of us exist bound by fear. Fear is the result of wrong patterns of thinking. Fear occurs when your habits and behavior spiral out of control and reveal to you things about the world that are false. Fear is an acronym for False Evidence Appearing Real. When you have control over your patterns of thinking and acting, you will know no fear. God has no fear as part of His being of Spirit. He cannot. Fear is ignorance, and God is knowledge. In second Timothy 1:7, Scripture says, "For God hath not given us the spirit of fear; but of power, and of love, and of a sound mind." God and fear cannot co-exist. Therefore when you are in God consciousness, you cannot feel fear.

Children are like blank pieces of paper, waiting for life's experience to imprint upon them.

Ernest Holmes and Raymond Charles Barker, two of our greatest spiritual scholars, have said that the reward for fear can be only negative, so fear is never a virtue. Yet fear sins twice: once in driving our own negative results, and again in teaching fear to our children. Children are like blank pieces of paper, waiting for life's experience to imprint upon them. If we are cautious and live in fear, we teach timidity and fear to our offspring. "In our early years, we have little or no control over what our consciousness is because our parents dominate our lives," writes Joel Goldsmith, "and in a sense they set the pattern of our consciousness so that we really are the showing forth of their states of consciousness. They imbue us with their standards, attitudes, and prejudices."

Inner Alchemy

Patterns can make us feel hopeless, because they appear to be so difficult to change. We develop habits over years and decades. The neural pathways in our brains become set and deeply impressed, driving us back to the same ideas, the same behaviors, again and again. Even unhealthy habits like smoking or overspending are hard to break. So can we actually change the patterns of our lives?

Yes, but not in an instant. Self-help literature is filled with the misleading advice that we can change overnight by sheer act of will, but that is false. Changing life's patterns requires dedicated effort, time and patience using a kind of inner alchemy. First we change our perception of reality and begin to see the truth of God's economy, and our patterns of thinking change slowly over time. What begins in the unconscious migrates into the conscious mind and thought begins to change outward action. We don't see the machinery of this change, only the results, but the machinery is always in operation. In time, the truths you know will become the harmonies that you manifest, and behavior will change.

This alchemic change in thinking also affects our relationships with others. We are creatures of thought, and our thoughts project outward at the quantum level to become causal agents in reality. Two people's thought patterns merge and mingle when they meet, and if they are tuned to the same frequency, those people will remain in contact and form a bond. If they are too opposed in their thinking, they will repel each other—not get along, as we like to say. This is why you will attract people into your sphere of influence who are like you: their thoughts vibrate on the same level as yours. Again we see it: like attracts like. I like to say that you are who you associate with, because each associate is an accurate reflection of the thoughts occurring in your own mind.

I Think, Therefore I Am

The great philosopher Rene Descartes meant that statement as a way of knowing that he really did exist. If he was able to ask the question, then his existence in the world had to be a reality. We take the phrase to mean something different: how you think determines who you are. You are a self-fulfilling prophecy. Whatever you think about in your subconscious eventually filters up to your conscious mind and has a causal effect on your reality, shaping who and what you are. So when you identify your patterns, you will know who you are.

So when you identify your patterns, you will know who you are.

ⵕ ⵕ ⵕ

This is true for all humans in this world. We all move in individual and collective patterns of thought that intersect and influence each other, like the patterns of concentric ripples from multiple rocks thrown in a pond. An example is success and failure, which tend to influence each other and feed off one another and bring each other into existence. Failure often breeds success as it changes our patterns of thinking to avoid past errors. Success can breed failure as our patterns shift again toward complacency or arrogance. Nothing is isolated. Everything is a constantly moving, evolving system of thought that takes us to a predictable end. If you know the pattern, you can predict the end. This is how the prophets do their work. We have honed our skills in identifying the hidden patterns of individual thought.

This does not mean that we are prisoners of our patterns, however. That would be like saying an obese woman can never lose weight because she can never alter her patterns of eating. What's needed is deliberate action and choice. You must interrupt the "business as usual" action of a cycle of behavior and make a deliberate, conscious change if you hope to bring about a new outcome. In this way you gain control over your destiny, as God intended. In this way do we turn free will into truth.

Gratitude Re-Envisioned

In the last chapter, we talked about the power of gratitude to reshape reality. Gratitude also has the ability to refocus your mind. Being grateful eliminates negative thoughts from your mind, and negative thinking is the bane of your existence. How many times have you gotten into a negative thought pattern and had something bad happen? Did you really believe that you were thinking that occurrence into

Nothing is random.

ා ා ා

being? You probably thought it was random chance, but it was not. Nothing is random. Everything is the result of thought, and patterns in your life are the direct outgrowth of your thinking, positive or negative.

Gratitude also has the power to attract good into your life by repelling negative thought and replacing it with kindness, compassion and awareness of your own good fortune. You have always had this good trying to reach you, but when your thoughts are negative they act as a shield that keeps good fortune from being able to reach your awareness. John Randolph Price wrote that, "Gratitude not only eliminates negative patterns caused by ingratitude, but it also works with the Law of Attraction to bring to you that which has already been tagged with your name, i.e. the good that your Spirit has already manifested for your 'life more abundant' but which your lower vibration has repelled."

You must consciously set the stage for this kind of change so your patterns can be changed. This is no accident. The pattern of abundance is not easy to set, because you have to do more than behave in a way that invites abundance; you need to *become* abundance. As John Randolph Price wrote, "You have now set the stage in consciousness to begin living as Abundance, and until the vibration is complete and in a permanent holding pattern, you will live only the Identity of Abundance. Your Higher Self is now the Master of Abundance and your lower nature is the channel for Abundance." It takes the conscious act of changing your patterns to achieve this state of being that transcends the mere act of thought. You must internalize the truth that you are your thoughts. You are a thought crystallized and expressed in flesh.

Whatever You Can Imagine

That is a huge, vast thought. You can become abundance, and when you do reach that exalted state you will be free of the chains of supply. But how do we get to that stage when we're beginning from such a place of ingrained behavior and human limits as we perceive them? One way is by visualization. Visualization is the imagination brought to a laser focus to bring that which is visualized into being. Visualization has enormous power. Health literature is full of cases in which patients who had been told they had cancer spent months in intense meditation, visualizing a white light penetrating their bodies and burning up their cancer, or patients with liver or kidney disease visualizing their immune systems destroying the diseased cells only to have medical scans reveal that the cancer was gone or the incurable disease had healed against all odds. The imagination has incredible power to tap into the reality of thought.

However, even imagination is confined to patterns. These patterns are different for each person, but awake or dreaming, our imaginations tend to wander the same routes: riches, terrors, or mundane matters.

Even daydreams follow a script. But as with conscious thought, we can alter our imaginary patterns with conscious effort. The only law is that everything must follow a pattern; what kind of pattern is open to interpretation. Within the structure, we have infinite freedom.

Within the structure, we have infinite freedom.

ᕲ ᕲ ᕲ

As you can see, man has the liberty to determine his own destiny by making deliberate changes to his pattern. No other creature on earth has this ability; all others are bound into patterns chiseled in stone and wound into the coils of their DNA. For us alone has God set the rules, pushed things into motion and turned us, His spiritual proxies, loose to see how we would react to the realities around us and evolve in the direction of God consciousness. We are the architects of our destinies, the authors of our advancement. Our stumbles and falls are not excused, but they are not unexpected, either; nothing is certain save the Laws that even God must follow. But in the end, we seem to remember our Divine nature and slowly ascend toward "I Am."

The Acorn and the Oak

You can imagine the power of the pattern by thinking about the oak tree and the acorn that it springs from. The actual oak does not reside in the acorn; it is far too large. Instead, the pattern that will eventually guide matter and energy to form an oak tree lives in the acorn, and it is this pattern that over time creates the huge tree from a tiny seed. The same could be said of any living thing with DNA: the pattern becomes the reality given time.

So is it with us and our minds. The patterns in our thinking drive matter and energy to create our reality. What you think of creates the condition that brings that thought into being. The more you think of it, the more pervasive it becomes in your experience. If you think promiscuous thoughts, you will find yourself mingling among people who will corrupt your moral code, leading to illicit and even dangerous sexual behavior. In this way, oral sex becomes a discourse between people who have pictured themselves as promiscuous. Thought pattern drives activity and attracts certain people into your radius.

The issue of attracting certain types of people is a great concern. People will often determine your potential and opportunity. We are all creatures of thought and mind, so our thinking reaches out to our brothers and sisters in a way that it does not to any other aspects of reality. We can make or break our fortunes by how we shape our thinking and what kind of people we attract to ourselves. This is why you must always have a destination in mind for yourself and then disseminate your thoughts with great care and discretion. They will bring into your awareness what you send out, even if they are weak or subconscious thoughts, over time they will attract what you secretly wish. Wish for greater, higher ends.

Wish for greater, higher ends.

ㅇ ㅇ ㅇ

Smashing the Mold of Your Thinking

Patterns are enduring things. Give them enough time to rattle around in the brain and they will solidify, codify into a sort of mold for the mind that restricts and binds its activity. Your mind makes the mold that shapes your experience. It actually limits the kinds of experiences you can have by limiting the paths your thoughts can tread. This mold shapes the incoming energies of the cosmos into the experiences you are having right now. It limits what they can be, how they can manifest. Think of Play-Doh from when you were a child, pushed through one of those molds that was shaped like a star. No matter what shape you tugged and pounded the Play-Doh into, it always came out a star on the other end. The mold determined everything.

But we have already learned that God's economy is not one of limitation but of endless supply, right? So any mold that limits what you can experience must be by nature unnatural, in defiance of God's intent. In that case, your mold is defective and much be destroyed. It can't be repaired. You can't go back and change patterns that are already set; you have to wipe them out and replace them. That is the only way you can prevent the flaw in the mold from continuing to affect you and shape your experience. Smash the mold and start anew!

You must smash the pattern of your present life.

☾ ☾ ☾

Vernon Howard relates a sort of parable about this act: "A manufacturer had a pattern by which he created a special kind of towel for the beach. The pattern produced defective towels. The manufacturer broke the pattern. No more defective towels appeared. You must break the pattern. You must smash the pattern of your present life. There is no use trying to repair the pattern. It cannot be repaired, for defects are everywhere. It must be broken and tossed out once and for all."

Subconscious thought created your pattern, but the subconscious in the end is subject to the rule of the conscious mind. To break the mold and create a new one, you must take conscious action that will lead to changes in your subconscious mind. This means adopting new habits, new patterns of thought and behavior. Persistent thought patterns turn into habits over time, and in this way we change our lives. It's not easy; "old habits die hard" is a truism for a good reason. But it can be done. People throw old habits over the side of the ship every day and replace them with new patterns that guide them toward the lives they desire.

These repeated positive actions—stating your "I Am," showing compassion for others, changing who you associate with, developing your entrepreneurial ideas—reshape your subconscious. Need proof? Think about driving a car. When you were learning to drive, you had to consider every action. You were unsure, so you weighed every choice in your conscious mind. But as time passed, the act of driving became habitual and your subconscious took over. Now when you drive, 90% of the time your subconscious is in command. Driving is habitual. The only time your conscious mind takes over is when you have to make a decision, such as when you are following directions. In this way, conscious action, repeated over time, imprints a new pattern on the inner, deeper mind.

Every day, you should be adding positive habits to your life. Make them part of your routine. Ingrain them in your mind. Over time, they will become your subconscious and you will begin to see the things that manifest in your life begin to change for the better.

The Alchemy of Faith

Thoughts are one aspect of Mind; feelings are another. While thoughts are the force that drives pattern development and the manifestation of your desires, feelings are harbingers. Deep feelings forecast what you are establishing in your mind as the cause for what you want to create. Do you feel anger? That will be the cause for what manifests in your corporeal reality, and it will likely be combative and conflicted.

Do you feel a passion for discovery and the hunger for knowledge? Then you will manifest learning, perhaps a university scholarship. Feelings are maps to what we are broadcasting to the energies of the universe at large.

But the ultimate aspect of Mind is belief. It is more powerful than thought or feeling. Belief represents the God potential within man. There has been much debate over the necessity for belief in religion; are not good works enough? Is belief necessary at all? If so, then is God a narcissist who simply wants flattery? Those questions miss the point of belief entirely because they stem from a place of ignorance of God's economy. In reality, God potential rests within you, your Divine potential. As a co-creator with God, God's power to deliver your desire is based on the strength of your belief. If you believe without reservation that your mind is one with His Mind, then you can achieve anything. If you believe less, you will achieve less.

If you believe less, you will achieve less.

∾ ∾ ∾

Belief has such might because it is the perfect, unquestioning acceptance that you are what you seek. You are already everything you need and desire, and you have always been thus. But until you accept and know it in your mind, it cannot come to pass. When you believe with all your Spirit, everything comes to pass. Faith is alchemy with the power to transform anything. In communion, the bread and wine truly become the body and blood of the Lord, as long as there is faith. Without faith, the church is lying. True faith does not question the ability of Mind and thought to create reality; it is the Mind that brings them into being.

So you are your own teacher of belief. You have the sole ability to transform your mind into a center of belief. The word *education* comes from the Latin "educo," meaning "to happen from the inside." You are your teacher. Only you can train yourself to develop that pattern of perfect belief and to become the change you seek.

A Brief Biology Break

The brain, while it is merely the transmitter and receiver of the Mind, still plays a vital role in the development of thought and consciousness. It's a marvelously complex and subtle machine, the seat of reason and the source of intention and emotion. In additon, the apex of the brain, known as the crown chakra, is the wellspring of the patterns that govern our actions. Charles Fillmore saw this reflected in the biblical story of Moses: "The Lord commanded Moses to 'make all things according to the pattern that was showed thee in the mount.' This 'mount' is the place of high understanding, or spiritual consciousness, whose center of action is in the very apex of the brain."

You must feel each part of your Spirit...

☺ ☺ ☺

In developing mental patterns that bring you into God consciousness, you need to align your seven charkas with God's energies. You do this by becoming quiet and still and listening to the voice of God speaking in your innermost mind, then attuning your Spirit to that speech. You must feel each part of your Spirit, represented by those seven areas, becoming a willing partner in setting aside the visible and material for the limitless and invisible. When you do this, you are in touch with that mental apex, the source of transcendent thinking. You will discover the deeper patterns of your nature—original thought patterns that came directly from the Mind of God. You will have begun your journey as part of the One Mind.

Those people who cannot tap their apex, whose egos prevent them from silencing what they think they know in their conscious experience and listening to God, end up in conflict. God's original thought patterns and the warring, jarring thoughts of a mind in conflict with itself will repel each other. Mental conflict is when your mind and God's Mind are operating on opposing planes. It becomes as if the lines are down between you and your Divine supply. Nothing comes into your life the way you desire.

It Is Done

The inherent warning is whatever you think, your mind builds. Work begins immediately; there are no permits required, no contractors to hire. Good or bad, the building starts as soon as you think it. As soon as you think about something, it is done. There is no way to take it back. So you've got to think with care! Here, the affirmation becomes a vital tool in disciplining your mind. Develop a phrase that you can repeat to yourself whenever you feel your mind backsliding into toxic thoughts, something like this from Jack and Cornelia Addington's *I Am the Way:*

ᘯ ᘯ ᘯ

I TURN AWAY FROM PATTERNS OF PAST FAILURES.
ALL THE POWER IN THE UNIVERSE IS MINE TO USE.
THE INFINITE INTELLIGENCE IN ME WILL
GUIDE ME TO SURE SUCCESS.

ᘯ ᘯ ᘯ

Over time, such deliberate thoughts will reshape your subconscious in the same way that regular lifting of weights will build muscle. The spiritual strength that you will acquire will be its own reward. The alternative is that you remain your out of control, poverty-inducing thoughts. No matter what you do, all your thoughts are acted upon. There is no negotiating of this law, no reversing it. Your thoughts will *always* set forces in motion. You must use your mind with care and maturity.

Holy Hellraisers

Responsible thinking is essential because it is those people who break patterns who move human society and the human condition forward. Moral courage is the province of righting wrongs, but creative courage is the art of seeing new patterns—new ways in which man can find truth and achieve God consciousness. This leads to the discovery of new symbols and forms, the foundation of a new society. The courage to shatter old patterns and see the new is the gift of the prophet. Do you have what it takes to become a prophet?

> *Do you have what it takes to become a prophet?*
>
> ☾ ☾ ☾

It is the job of the prophet to stir up controversy. Change, even if its goal is to bring man closer to his natural Divine state, is always met with resistance. People will always resist change, and it is a hallmark of the "holy hellraiser" that his or her effort is met with more resistance the more Divine his connection to the universe is. Artists, musicians, writers, activists—the ones who stir things up and create anger are the ones who are trying to advance their people! That is why you should never oppress artists, but always make way for them to speak. Artists possess the vision of prophets, that touch of the transcendent sight that some mistake for insanity but you can now recognize as the vision of God's economy. Artists create hope for the people to grab onto so they can rise up and change the way they think. Hellraisers challenge us and make us change how we think. That is their purpose.

What is the difference between black leaders and leading blacks? Black leaders come from the tradition of the people, so they understand the thought patterns that have kept blacks limited. More importantly, they have overcome those patterns. They promote individual progress, but not necessarily the progress of the race. On the other hand, leading blacks are pure self-promotion. They look like you, but they don't think like you! They are manipulators, hired by oppressors to push an agenda, to anger you over the trivial and distract you from the truth that you must take control of your mind to take control of your destiny.

Learn to recognize the false prophets and false leaders and you will also know the true hellraisers, those who can inspire you to greater vision.

Everything Starts With the Mind

Charles Fillmore writes, "God is never absent from you. He is constantly taking form in your life according to the exact pattern of your words, thoughts, and actions. Just as soon as you really bring your words and your expectations up to the measure of God's love for you, you will demonstrate." God will bring you what you think, no more, no less. He is your source of your own manifestation. You are responsible for all that comes into your life, just as the adult child, not his parent, is responsible for his decisions.

This is an invigorating reality, because there are no scapegoats. We hold all the cards and all the keys. Sick thought patterns will lead to illness. Powerless thought patterns will lead to our power being stripped from us. Everything we think will be expressed in our circumstances.

Nona Lavell Brooks, the brilliant co-founder of Divine Science, expressed it thus:

"The way we grow and release ourselves from our limited experiences is by the changing of our thought patterns. Each unfoldment of thought is a resurrection. Out of some dead concept, our mentality rises to a greater realization of the living Truth. The more conscious we are of the Truth of Life, the fuller our understanding of the forms of life. It is man's thought of life that awakens in consciousness to fuller comprehension of what is. The revelation of truth by which man sees more and more clearly is evolution. We ascend to realize our perfect Self, the Christ. All things await man's recognition and acceptance."

Change your pattern of attraction and you will change your world. This is why Jesus commands us to love our enemies—not because they necessarily deserve love, but because every thought pattern of love, abundance, health or justice that we express into the cosmos evokes a higher function of the Laws of Being on our behalf. When we change our patterns of thinking, we attract God to us. We carry ourselves to higher and higher levels of consciousness. We begin to claim the Divine legacy that our Father has set down for each of us. Praise God.

11

— THE LAW OF GOAL ACHIEVEMENT —

꧇ ꧇ ꧇

Energy is the essence of life. *Every day you decide how you're going to use it by knowing what you want and what it takes to reach that goal, and by maintaining focus.*

—*Oprah Winfrey*

The self-help world is full of talk about goals. You're to set goals, focus on goals, achieve goals, plan for goals, write down goals and on and on. But what is a goal and why is it important? A goal is nothing less than a fulcrum for your mind, a base that your mind can use to move the universe.

We've discussed at great length how you already possess every-thing you desire in your own consciousness. But we have yet to talk about your means of channeling and focusing that consciousness. After all, it's a truth that even the most effective tool, improperly used, is worthless. So you must focus your powerful consciousness in order for it to bring forth the ends you desire from the cosmos. Goals are your way of turning your mind, which is so occupied with the day-to-day demands of living, into a laser that brings you the ultimate results you desire. Goal achievers find life, and yet they do not boast. Boasting is for empty souls; goal achievers are happy and content in their place in God's reality. They enjoy the satisfaction of knowing they are using their minds to their fullest. On the other hand, if you do not have goals, you will likely end up very frustrated in life. Your Divine mind will wander aimlessly and you will achieve little beyond the sweat of your brow.

Health, Wealth and Happiness

Who does not want these things? Who does not wish to be healthy, prosperous and joyful in each and every day? No one! We all want to live long lives filled with security, pleasure and love. Yet not all of us do. In fact, I would argue that few of us really do this. The majority of people seek out a living and live according to their lack, not the abundance that dwells within them. They suffer from poor health and spend much of their time resenting those who enjoy greater material wealth than they do. But this is not how man was meant to live.

> *God did not place us in this reality to suffer!*
> ☽ ☽ ☽

God did not place us in this reality to suffer! He gave us all the tools we need to manufacture our health, wealth and happiness out of the raw stuff of spiritual energy: our Divine mind, our will and our total faith in Him. We need no other currency. Yet most human beings do not live in this economy. They dwell instead in a system of lost jobs, shrinking paychecks, scant healthcare and continual worry. They do so for a simple devastating reason: *they do not see themselves as the cause of their problems.* The fact is very basic:

NO ONE CAN DO ANYTHING TO YOU
THAT YOU DO NOT ALLOW.

ↄ ↄ ↄ

We are our own worst enemies. We sabotage our own prosperity and happiness by getting lazy, by focusing our attention on meager, small things, by getting hooked on drugs or booze or sex or gambling, or simply by thinking only about what we do not have instead of what we can create. Goal setters don't do this. Instead, they are self-aware. They see that they are the cause of their problems, and this awareness empowers them to identify themselves as the solution. This is what allows them to set goals that focus the mind and lead to happiness, plenty and long life.

Goals Are the Stuff of Design

For enlightened individuals who are fully cognizant of God's Laws and the mind-based nature of reality, setting goals is as natural as breathing. It is a habit, and as Aristotle said, we are our habits. The most successful people in the world—captains of industry, entrepreneurs, great artists, top athletes—are all compulsive goal setters. When they start each day, they have goals in mind they want to accomplish by the end of that day. They also set weekly, monthly and yearly goals. You can imagine how this constant goal setting hones the mind and the "I Am" nature of the consciousness to a razor edge. Goal setters are always zeroed in on a specific objective, bringing that result into physical manifestation out of the limitless possibilities of the cosmos.

This is the essence of "intelligent design." We're not talking about an alternative to evolution, but about how intelligent, enlightened beings design their own reality by imposing their goal-focused will upon it. Goal setting, and the following of those goals with "I Am" statements, applied will and relentless activity, turns potential into actual. It is both art and science and—this is vitally important—it is not luck or chance. Goal achievement is governed by the mental laws of the universe; there is no luck involved. Another way of saying this would be that we create our own luck, or that "fortune favors the prepared."

This is life-changing! Am I saying that by setting specific goals for your life, you can take what appears to be luck or chance out of the equation and have control over what you can earn, how you can live and how healthy you can be? YES! That is precisely the message of this chapter. There is no luck or chance; there are only results that you attract to yourself by what you think and how your consciousness interacts with the reactive substrate of reality. Reality reacts to your state of mind in the same way that another person reacts to your touch. Touch another with love or hope and they will respond in kind; reach out in anger and you're likely to get a fist in return. Reality is a psycho-reactive substance, and if you leave things to chance, it will send you results taken from an infinite supply of strange, frightening and confounding possibilities. But when you set goals, you impose *order* on that reality! You direct its energies and bring to you the results that you desire. Goals are a lens to focus your mind and direct the universe to bring you what you want when you are ready for it.

> *Reality reacts to your state of mind in the same way that another person reacts to your touch.*
>
> ୨ ୨ ୨

A Law of Mind

Jack Addington wrote, "The words conceive, believe, and receive are inscribed on the gold medallion worn by many students of Abundant Living, and are the abbreviation of a very important law. We call it the law of goal-achievement. For, it is a law of mind that that which you can conceive of, believe in, and confidently expect for yourself, must necessarily become your experience."

Goal achievement is a law of the mind. This is why the greatest teachers and minds of our time talk about why goal setting is so vital to personal performance and success. You won't find one who doesn't counsel you to set goals. Why is that? Because as Jack wrote, goals distill in your mind what you can achieve and make you believe that you can become what you desire. Think about the process of goal setting. You might make a list of the goals you intend to reach in a given year: double your income, buy a new house, lose 30 pounds. When you consider these goals and set them in stone and work to achieve them, you are really bargaining with yourself as to what you believe you can accomplish. When you reach a point where you state, "I Am these goals and I will reach them," you are deciding what you can achieve. You are defining your own limits in that time period!

Goal achievement is a law of the mind.

❍ ❍ ❍

This is why I always counsel people to set audacious goals. Not nice goals, not big goals, but *audacious* goals. Set goals so grand and great that other people gasp for breath and tell you that you're crazy. Why? Because the goal you accept for yourself defines what you believe you can achieve, and that belief is what sets the cosmic economy in motion to deliver what you mind asks for. Ask small and you'll get small, but why do that? Ask for the great and glorious and God's system will bring it to you. Audacious goals stretch you and put you out on that edge where all you can rely on is the Divine economy of Mind and faith. And let me tell you, God loves those who live on the edge and rely on Him for their means.

The goals you can reach will depend entirely on that which you can imagine for yourself...

Goal achievement depends entirely on you. The goals you can reach will depend entirely on that which you can imagine for yourself and believe that you can achieve, because that thing will become your experience. If it wasn't clear before, let's make it clear now: *God does not bring you anything but the means to gift yourself with the life you desire.* God is not a giver of rewards. He is a giver of means and tools and inspiration. When you use the tools He provides, such as informed goal achievement, you will earn for yourself the rewards that His system makes possible.

You Are the Master

So we're on our own. God isn't going to bail you out if you decide to screw up your life. He's not going to send an angel to grab that bottle out of your hand or separate you from that person who's about to ruin your marriage. God is not Big Brother. He's the Source, not the puppet master. You are your own master. Your will and self-determination power the Law of Goal Achievement.

Will and self-determination go hand in hand in achieving your goals. Rather than imposing your will upon the world, I mean that you must set your goals, then have the will to follow through not only on the mindset of "I Am what I have set as my goal," but on the actions that are required to bring that goal to fruition. If your goal is to start a new company, you must go out and till the soil and self-determine how that goal will take shape. The universe will bring you the raw material of your goal, but your actions determine its form. So you must go out and find good people to work in your company, develop your ideas, and put yourself in a position so that when your goal begins to manifest, you are ready to receive it.

While you do this, it is vital that you do not lose sight of the power your consciousness has to foster or sidetrack your goals. You must become a master of your thoughts and feelings, keeping your mind centered on the coming reality of your goals and your worthiness to achieve them. You must always continue to believe that you will achieve your goals, for belief keeps that all-important mental energy flowing. This can be difficult as you are learning to control random thoughts and deal with doubts, so in the beginning especially, I suggest that you use meditation and prayer to concentrate your mind and reach that state of total belief and total acceptance. Pray and meditate regularly on your goals and your ability not only to reach them, but to become them. This kind of self-mastery is one of the highest achievements to which a person can aspire.

Breaking Barriers

Addington writes, "Mental barriers to goal achievement should be rooted out as soon as possible if we would become goal achievers." That is the best advice you could receive. We all erect mental barriers to our own successes. Some are born from our upbringing, when we were told we could not achieve something. Some come from experiencing failure in life and internalizing it, convincing ourselves that failure is part of who we are. Others stem from listening to the ill advice of others, people who are relentlessly negative and discourage us. From all these sources mental barriers are erected from the brick of fear and the mortar of self-doubt and apathy.

But failure is optional. No one is cursed. No one is destined to fail. You create your own destiny. Therefore, barriers can be broken. And if you are to realize your goals, you must break them. Ask yourself, what is keeping you from doing what you know you were ordained by God to do? Fear? A false sense of duty? Resignation that "things will never change?" You must shatter those mental barriers immediately, and do it ruthlessly. If you have friends who consistently fill your mind with negative thoughts, abandon them. This is a matter of survival, and friends who make you less than you who can become are not friends at all. If you have habits that are leading you to achieve less than your potential, change them radically, right now! Do something extreme in your day and leave old habits behind.

No one is destined to fail.

∽ ∽ ∽

You must also shed what I call your "coat of many excuses." Joseph had his coat of many colors, but it pales in significance to the excuses many of us wear. Why didn't we achieve the things we were capable of? We got sidetracked. We didn't graduate high school. We got married. Someone stole our idea. We don't know, we just didn't do it. There are more excuses in this world than stars in the heavens, and you know what? God ain't listening. He doesn't care about excuses.

The universe doesn't care about excuses. Excuses exist for one reason and one reason alone:

○ ○ ○

TO GIVE US THE ILLUSION THAT SOME OUTSIDE FORCE IS TO BLAME FOR OUR FAILURES.

○ ○ ○

That's so we can live with the *guilt* of not becoming what we know we should have become! So we can exist with the titanic, monstrous regret of missing out on our calling. That's a sad, meager way to live. Drug addicts make excuses. Wife beaters and criminals make excuses. Losers make excuses. Goal achievers take responsibility for their mistakes, become aware that they are the cause of their troubles, and set their minds to changing things. They exhibit the three Ps, the three Divine characteristics that unlock the economy of the Lord:

○ ○ ○

PATIENCE. PERSISTENCE. PERSEVERANCE.

○ ○ ○

In James 1:3, the Bible says that you must prove yourself through the trying of your faith. That means you will be tested. Your will and determination to reach your goals and bring them into being will be tested by adversity, jealousy, self-doubt and misfortune. Everyone is tested this way! I have been tested this way! There is no great leader, no billionaire, no Pulitzer-winning writer or champion athlete who has not had his or her faith tested on the road to achievement.

It's human nature to become too complacent when success comes too easily. We can become too sure of ourselves, overconfident and think, "Hey, I've got this manifestation thing wired." Tests of faith hone and sharpen your will, patience, persistence and perseverance to a fine edge and remind you never to let your mind become lazy. In fact, tests and trials make you stronger, help you refine your ideas and increase your determination. The road to success and happiness cannot ever be smooth; it must be riddled with the vagaries of life that define who we become. When we can prove our faith, we will want for nothing.

A Cup of "Expresso"

If consciousness is the engine by which the substance of the universe is stimulated to bring forth material reality, then goals are the steering wheel for that consciousness. But why is this the case? Why should the focus of goals bring forth such a powerful reaction from the unseen realms?

Because the activity of our minds is merely a reflection of the Divine Mind in its constant striving to express itself through us on the material plane. Remember, God is pure Spirit; He cannot express Himself directly on the material world, but must act through humans in Spirit. So His every moment is a conscious act of expression through us, His creations. Our very thoughts are the offspring of Divine thought seeking a doorway to be fully expressed and realized. The cosmos itself is a cosmos of self-expression. The Intelligence that underlies all reality and makes consciousness the fundamental force of existence is an expressive, mobile Intelligence. The universe is not static; it needs to be expressed.

The universe is not static; it needs to be expressed.

ᘮ ᘮ ᘮ

That expression is your purpose for being. You exist as one small part of the wholeness of God's intended expression of His being in the material world. Your thought is the outlet through which God sends that expression, yet because you have free will, He cannot express Himself unless your consciousness allows it. This is the reason why it is so vital to learn to control your thoughts and dwell only on the things that you want to experience. You must train your mind as a martial arts black belt trains his hands and feet: to shed doubt, fear, want and thoughts of lack, and to think only about becoming the blessings that you seek and knowing without doubt that they are on the way into your experience. This is mental discipline that can take years to master, but the payoff is the health, wealth and happiness that we all desire.

As Carol Sheffield writes, "We must learn to control our thinking, for this is the great secret of achievement in mental work. We should think that which we wish to experience."

The Art of the Goal

The achievement of a cherished goal is a planned event, not happenstance. It comes about because you understand the Laws and follow these critical steps:

1. Choosing your audacious goal.

2. Believing completely in your ability to achieve it.

3. Stating that you ARE that goal to the cosmos.

4. Acting in accordance with your goal to prepare yourself to receive it.

5. Training your mind to reject doubt going forward.

When you plan for these needs and address them in your mind, you make goal achievement inevitable. You are acting and being according to the Laws of Being and God's system for reward and abundance. You do not need to let your mind be subject to the whims of chance; you can plan your thinking and govern your consciousness to bring about the results you desire. This is what the Bill Gates and Oprah Winfreys of the world do. They don't allow doubt to seep in—they banish it and stay focused on their goals! It's when you can't do this that you bring misfortune down on your head. As the King James Bible says, in Proverbs 26:2, "As the bird by wandering, as the swallow by flying, so the curse causeless shall not come." Every curse has a cause. We are our own best allies and potential worst enemies. We choose which.

In the same way, goal achievement does not come without years of practice. As I said earlier, training your mind to focus on goals and exclude doubt is like a martial artist earning a black belt. No karate student earns a black belt in weeks or months; it takes years of work and study. Goal achievement is only achieved through practice, through repetitious work on governing your mind to make it do what you want: choose goals, believe in them, become them with total faith and confidence, and control stray thoughts that can shipwreck your plans. Practice is the price of proficiency at goal achievement. The more you practice, the better you will become at bringing desires into manifestation with the power of your mind. Eventually, with enough work, it will become like breathing to you. Practice makes permanent.

> *We are our own best allies and potential worst enemies.*
>
> ဥ ဥ ဥ

What Dreams May Come

James Allen writes, "The greatest achievement was at first and for a time a dream. The oak sleeps in the acorn; the bird waits in the egg; and in the highest vision of the soul a waking angel stirs." So it is, for all things begin in the mind as dreams or ideas. Nothing starts otherwise. All inventions, sonnets, symphonies, companies, political movements, breakthroughs and families began as dreams in the minds of those who eventually brought them into being. All reality is the product of thought made manifest.

> *Every achievement begins as a dream.*
> ୨ ୨ ୨

Think about that if you doubt what I say. Once, the book you read did not exist. Then I decided to write it. I wrote it on a computer that was invented by another person who saw in his mind how such a machine could come to be. It was printed by another machine that began as a thought, and so on. Everything you see or experience began as a thought either in the mind of God or man. Every achievement begins as a dream. The question is, when your dream comes, will you honor it and bring it into being or reject it as impossible and kill it before it can even be born?

This is why it becomes so essential to your future prosperity to learn the power of directed thought. James Allen writes, "All achievements, whether in the business, intellectual, or spiritual world, are the result of definitely directed thoughts." Directed thought is a level beyond merely controlling your thoughts, as we have talked about earlier. Controlling thoughts means you don't allow negative thoughts to reach into the ether and derail what you have coming toward you, but there's not much control beyond that. It's like caging your thoughts. Directed thought opens the cage and lets the wild horse out, but rides the horse, directing your mighty thoughts to achieve specific effects or results in your conscious experience.

Directing your thoughts is powerful discipline, the black belt of manifestation. In doing so, you channel the power of your mind toward a precise goal, such as raising $1 million to launch a new company. You see the goal achieved in your mind, become that million dollars via your believing "I Am" declaration, and then keep your mind directed to the realization of that becoming state until it comes into your reality. Your directed thoughts fan out into the psycho-reactive substrate that is reality and shape that million dollars out of the stuff of spirit and send it your way. With enough focus, the money comes to you! The same can be said for opportunity, a house, a relationship or health. Direct your thoughts and change your world.

Creatures of Imagination

A philosopher once speculated that humans continued to exist through nothing more than sheer will, and that is not far off. We are not creatures of will, but of imagination. Neville wrote that "The eternal body of man is the imagination." Imagination, said William Blake, is the gateway of reality. Thought and imagination hold the key to all achievement, because we are ultimately beings of thought rather than matter. Matter is just a housing for the minds that connect us to the cosmos.

This is why it is important, as you move forward in your development of your consciousness and your ability to control and direct your thinking, to learn to stop caring about the outer world. It is the realm of Spirit and Mind that matter; the physical is an illusion. The path to wealth, health and happiness does not begin with the physical; it merely ends with it as your goals are fulfilled from the realm of Spirit.

So to achieve your greatest desires, you must occupy yourself entirely with the invisible world of Mind.

Joel Goldsmith writes, "In spite of how successful you may be in human achievement, you will never attain spiritual awareness. That comes only when you have 'died' to caring about the outer scene and are willing to take life as it is and work from within toward the goal of God-realization." This is not easy. We are programmed by our daily lives to put the outer world first—to concentrate on the next meal, our jobs, our exercise routine, our rent. It is understandable to think that success comes from somehow muddling through the mazes of the material world to scratch and claw to the top. But mental discipline means you must stop thinking of the physical as primary and realize that your physical self is only a host for your Spirit. Spirit is the prime mover of the world.

When you take this approach to life, you become, as Walt Whitman described, a conqueror of life, like Joshua or Caleb. You become one of those rare individuals who sees a mountain and says, "I will find a way to the top." When your imagination and Spirit are the core of your experience, there is no problem you cannot solve, because no solution is beyond the realm of the imagination. Sure, the solution might seem impossible, but doing the impossible is what makes great men great, and something is only impossible until it's achieved. Then it becomes inevitable. Flight was impossible until the Wright Brothers did it. Imagination conquers all.

Imagination conquers all.

Ͽ Ͽ Ͽ

God is the Goal

In the end, God awareness is your ultimate goal. Beyond material wealth, security, opulence, physical and mental health and the happiness that comes from helping others and making the world a better place lies God. God is both your means to achieve your goal (through His system) and the goal itself. What does that mean? It means that when your mind is perfectly attuned to the realm of Spirit, when your thoughts are directed like laser beams to the creation of everything you can imagine, then you will become One with God. You will have achieved that state of total expression that God desires. You become a transparent vessel that God can fill up with His vision and know that you will make that vision a reality on Earth.

You must know Truth of Being.

Charles Fillmore writes, "Everyone desires to be something beyond his present achievement. I tell you right now, you will never realize that ideal until you go **into** partnership with God. You must know Truth of Being. You must conform to Truth in every thought and in every act. Then you will have success. Then you will be satisfied. Then you will know that the Spirit of truth does demonstrate itself in man." It is your destiny to be a partner with God, to help Him create the world of His vision. We all desire to be better—better people, better spirits, better custodians of God's world, and in us the spirit of truth demonstrates itself. The truth of God's system, the power of thought and faith to transform our material reality before our eyes, exists in man and reveals itself every day in those of us who choose to follow God's Laws.

Vernon Howard writes, "One man was disturbed by believing that several friends criticized him behind his back. Whether they actually did or not is beside the point. The only point is his agitated reaction towards his own assumption. His disturbance appeared to throw out a chain which bound him to the others. The others had nothing to do with the chain; it was his own idea. What he must do, finally, is to simply have no concern with what others think of him. Achievement can come by replacing his fictitious self with his natural self. Nature is blissfully unconcerned."

The message is, do not worry about what others think. People are not the masters of the Law of Goal Achievement. God is. You bring about any positive or negative results you experience based on your thought. Choose to think from a place of power and you will achieve power. Choose impotence and that is what you will know. Nature remains unconcerned. A baby is unconcerned about being born naked; it knows that is how it was meant to be. Be as a child. You have only to be who you were ordained to be and nothing else matters. You always have the choice.

12

— THE LAW OF REVISION —

T̄he weak can never forgive. Forgiveness is the attribute of the strong.

—*Gandhi*

Forgiveness is central to Christianity. After all, through the sacrifice of Christ on the cross, we are all forgiven for our human transgressions and made heirs to the Kingdom of God. Yet that is not the kind of forgiveness I am talking about in this chapter. Here, we are going to examine the concept of revision—not in the sense of revising an essay or a term paper or whitewashing an unfortunate past, but in the sense of "re-visioning" your existence and your actions within the system laid down by God. In the Science of Being, "revision" means literally "to develop a new vision."

There are many translations and versions, but as you have read it, Proverbs 29:18 states that "Where there is no vision, the people perish." In ancient times that was true, because the leader of a clan or a city-state needed to have farseeing vision to plan for crop failures, plagues, invasions and other crises that could have killed his people. Today, those aren't our problems. Instead, today the Scripture might more accurately read, "Where there is no revelatory vision, the people are directionless." This means that unless you have a coherent vision of who you are and where you are going, you will wander aimlessly through life. You will never grasp the Laws of Being much less take your place in God's system of creation. You will be isolated from the true nature of God, and that is death in the spiritual sense. Death and Hell are separation from the Divine both in ourselves and in God.

The Nature of Forgiveness

So let us work on "re-visioning." One of the essential steps in this process is *self-forgiveness.* That's different than the forgiveness I spoke about at the start of the chapter. Through Christ, God has already forgiven you for your sins. Forgiving yourself for your past misjudgments, hurtful deeds and poor choices is another matter. We can be our own worst enemies and forgiving ourselves is often more difficult than forgiving others. But you can imagine how important this is when you are seeking a revision of your life and purpose. As Neville writes, "Revision is of greatest importance when the motive is to change oneself, when there is a sincere desire to be something different, when the longing is to awaken the ideal active spirit of forgiveness."

...learn to forgive yourself for your past and learn from it.

It is vital that as you enter the process of revision, you learn to forgive yourself for your past and learn from it. There is nothing you have done that cannot be healed and made right when you give yourself over to God's Laws. But to do this, you must accept that you are human and therefore flawed, and while you may not have an excuse for the errors of your past, you are not defined by them. As a wise man once said, you can't go back and rewrite the beginning of your story, but you can start now and rewrite the end.

Forgiveness is the beginning of revision, and after that it's a step-by-step process. You can't begin to revise your vision by re-imagining your entire self in one great mental leap; it's too much, too big, too daunting. You'll be overwhelmed by the task. No, the first step is to revise your day. How does this work? It's a very simple process:

1. Begin by looking at your day and taking account of the troubles and vexations that came your way.

2. Look with a critical eye at how you dealt with them.

3. Re-imagine how you could deal with them in a manner that is more in line with your new perception that Mind is everything and you have within you the Divine spark of creation.

4. Revise your vision of your day and resolve to apply that new vision when such troubles come your way in the future.

Every time you do this, you change your mind. You revise the way you think and implant the seed of a fresh vision of yourself in your consciousness. Every revision takes you a step closer to overcoming your fears, mastering your passions and changing your habitual way of approaching life. Rather than overwhelm yourself with a grand new vision of how your entire being must change at once, make each day an act of revision and learning and over time, you will cause yourself to evolve.

How Do You See?

The word "vision" can be deceiving. The eyes can deceive us as well. Revision is not a matter of seeing with the eyes. As we well know, optical illusions and our own cherished delusions can make us see what we wish to see rather than what is real. No, revision is a matter of seeing with the mind. Seeing only with the eye limits our vision to what is before us, and we know how limiting that can be. As William Blake put it, "We are led to believe a lie when we see with, not through, the eye."

To truly revision ourselves, the eye must become merely the doorway into the brain and mind. The true vision must occur in our consciousness as we use our renewed mind to see not what is in front of us, but what can be in our future—that which is not before our eyes but just beyond our personal horizon. Remember that the forces of the universe do not respond to want or thoughts of lack; they respond to mental images of what will be and what you will become. So if you trust only your physical eyes for your vision, and your life currently is one of want and meagerness, that vision will shape your result. You will see only what is in front of you, and it will be impoverished. Your revision will be the same.

Instead, see with your mind's eye: see in your consciousness what your world and future can become. See it as though it has already come to pass in your material experience. See your existence as it can be and declare it as it has already become in your mind. Then that vision crystallizes in reality and becomes Divine truth. You will begin to become what you have envisioned in this way—the person, the wealth, the state of health, the focus of mind. The eyes of the mind are infinitely sharper than those you see with on a daily basis. You need both sets, but do not let your long-term vision of yourself be defined by what your material eyes see.

The Law of Revision also requires you to undergo a change of heart, a radical redirection of your values and goals that instantly alters what you want from your life and how you see not only yourself but others. If this seems improbable, it only remains so until you wholly revision your existence and realize that you have been your own worst enemy until now. We sabotage our own Divine potential with greed, sloth, envy and other petty ways and when we see those ways laid bare, a change of heart often results. The Prodigal Son experienced such a sea change in his own ways when he came to himself.

> *The Law of Rsevision also requires you to undergo a change of heart.*
>
> ☾ ☾ ☾

This is what we call the Theology of Responsibility: understanding that God merely places and evokes potentials in us, but we make the decisions. We choose to follow the path of our potential or to deny it. And when we awaken to the fact that we have spent perhaps 40 years wasting our potential and denying God, the revelation is painful! This is why revision must happen gradually. It's not advisable to burden oneself with such overpowering guilt and regret all at once. Better to tackle one area of your life at a time than scream "J'accuse!" for your entire existence and sink into depression.

Such regret and anger does have its purpose, however. The process of revision can be challenging, because it forces us into our own private Hell, the awareness that we have been denying God and thus denying ourselves. But it takes this powerful emotion to drive people to have a change of heart. This is the inner battle that is fought in thought. Once we accept that we have failed in the past and come to terms with that truth, we can begin to see in our mind's eye what we can *become*—

and becoming is everything! Only after you have passed through this crucible will you be open to truly re-imagining yourself. As Neville writes, "The battle man fights is fought out in his own imagination. The man who does not revise the day has lost the vision of that life, into the likeness of which it is the true labor of the "Spirit of Jesus" to transform this life."

The Remains of the Day

In the end, revision is about taking the day just past and re-imagining it in a way that brings it into alignment with your overall Divine vision of how you want your world to take shape. Basically, you look back on what you would have done differently and make peace with the chaos of the day, seeing in your mind's eye how you could have made different choices. Over time, this action reshapes your pre-emptive actions, changing the choices you make in the days to come, or as Neville says, "modifies the trend of your life."

In this process, as in everything else, it all begins with thought and speech, so you must learn to govern your tongue. Never speak of anything in your day past as inevitable, or you risk setting that behavior in stone for yourself. Instead, regard your own character and nature as fluid, subject to your own will according to the Laws of God. This way, you'll avoid the trap of cementing bad habits or poor thoughts into place for years to come. Master your thoughts and you will make revision far easier and more rewarding.

Our good is buried in these revisions of our days. The days past are never perfect, but in revising them in our minds, we call forth the potential perfection that lies waiting in our future days. Revisioning your daily litany of choices, words, thoughts and actions allows you to mine the potential good from the time to come. Our potential good, the good that we can do for ourselves and others, waits for us to rise and do our best to bring it into fruition. It already exists, but it waits for our consciousnesses to pull it from the etheric into the actual. So in mentally rehashing what we have done with the day, we discover the kernels of future blessings and glory by becoming wiser and more knowing about ourselves and our ability to act according to the Laws. Romans 8:19 reads, "For the earnest expectation of the creature waiteth for the manifestation of the sons of God." Revisioning every day gives you the tools to manifest in future days.

Repent to Create Paradise

Ready to have your theological world rocked again? I haven't done it in a few chapters, and I don't want you to get too comfortable. So here's another challenge to the conventional way of thinking about God and Christianity: Heaven does not exist outside of yourself. That runs counter to what we have been told all our lives, but it's true. Heaven or Paradise are not external locations; they exist only within the Mind and the Spirit. When you revision your days, you are creating paradise one step at a time. Seeing the world

Heaven does not exist outside of yourself.

through your physical eyes leaves only a trace residue of the ugliness and pointlessness that can seem to be all around us. But when you see with your mind's eye and reshape the day according to your imagination of what it can become, you create that paradise in your mind.

However, adhering to the Law of Revision demands a change in your attitude toward everything. This differs from changing your awareness that Mind and thought are the currency of the Divine economy. That was an intellectual leap. The kind of change I'm talking about is emotional. It's about repentance. Now, repentance brings to mind visions of people testifying and begging forgiveness for their sins, but that's not the kind of repentance that's relevant here. Repentance in the Science of Being means a reversal of the attitudes with which you approach the world. When you can forgive yourself for your past actions and repent of your old way of seeing life, you will undergo a radical change of attitude.

> ## *The kind of change I'm talking about is emotional.*
>
> ᔅ ᔅ ᔅ

The world attitude is revealing: it can mean the angle at which a craft approaches its destination, such as the angle of flight of an aircraft. What angle are you taking as you approach your destination as the appointed custodian of part of God's vision for earth?

Repentance opens the gates to radical change and the creation of a new tone of reality. This is why the Law of Revision is so important: it addresses your past actions, acknowledging that they shape your future. In finance, there is a saying, "Past performance is not an indicator of future results," but we know that's largely untrue. Past performance usually does predict what you will do, unless you drastically alter your attitude and entire cognitive model for regarding the world and your place in it. This is also called a "paradigm shift."

When you can summon the courage to take a hard look at your past, put it to rest and find new eyes with which to see today and tomorrow, you can shape reality in a new way. Follow these steps:

• Think about your actions.

- Imagine acting or speaking differently until you experience the events differently in your mind.

- Continue until you are pleased or satisfied.

- You will have rewritten the events of the day.

This is not revisionist history or some kind of delusion that you practice to make yourself feel better or erase the troubles of the day. You know that mind is the energy source and prime mover of energy and matter and that mind determines what will enter your physical experience. So when you go back and reshape the events of the day with your mind, you can change what your mind set in motion that day! You can undo the past! With a radical change in attitude and a concentration on changing your mental experience, you can turn a day

You can undo the past!

ꙩ ꙩ ꙩ

mired in poverty or error into a day that contributes to your future wealth, health and happiness. Bishop Henry Brown believed that he could have air conditioning in his church at a time when no church in the nation had it. But he looked back in time and re-imagined his experience as though he had the cool breeze of air conditioning flowing over his grateful congregation. And lo and behold, it came to pass that his was the first church in the country to have air conditioning.

In this way we see another way in which science and God's Laws are alike: they are time independent. Quantum mechanics allows information to travel forward or backward in time, which is what makes precognition and prophecy possible. In the same way, God's laws allow us to go back and revise the signals we are sending to the spirit world from our thoughts and change our outcomes. As Neville wrote, I take my day and review it in my mind's eye. I start with the first incident in the morning and go through the day. When I come to any scene that displeases me, I stop right there and revise it. I rewrite it. After I have rewritten it so it conforms to my ideal, I experience it in my imagination as though I had experienced it in the flesh. I do it over and over until it takes on the tone of reality."

There's No One to Blame

If it hasn't been clear up to now, you haven't been paying attention: you are responsible. The Theology of Responsibility is absolute: God is the parent, but He is not directing your actions. No one is. The culture of victimhood has no validity in God's economy; there is no one else to blame for your bad outcomes and you deserve all the credit for your victories. When you think someone is to blame for something that went awry, you have a duty as an enlightened being to lift that man up and discover that he is not the root cause of your troubles. You are.

In this way, we discover that the world is a reflection of us, including all the people in our lives. Everything you experience comes from your mind and imagination. Therefore you are the source of everything that happens in your experience, good and bad. Your conversations also reflect this fundamental responsibility for your reality. Words have mass, form, energy and potency, and the substance of your conversations will shape what happens to you. If you want to create a vivid picture of paradise—wealth, health, joy and spiritual enlightenment—then begin by turning your words and conversations with others in the direction of prosperity and success.

> *Everything you experience comes from your mind and imagination.*
>
> ༺ ༒ ༻

Your conversations should correspond to your ideal beliefs and the kind of world you want to create for yourself. This is where "talking the talk" has greater strength than "walking the walk." Writes Neville, "Watch your conversations carefully; are they from premises of fulfilled desires? If they are not, go back and make them correspond to the ideal you want to embody in this world."

In sum, revision requires that you identify your mental activity in all states—memory, communication, cognition in the present, foresight—and tune it to the pitch of what you wish to realize in your world. Your life will reflect your thoughts; if your thoughts, words and conversations are of desperation, need and illness, that is what will come into your experience. If nothing good is happening in your life, there's nothing upstairs going on either! The external world is a *symptom* of your patterns of pervasive thinking, a shadow of your mental activity and your ability or lack thereof to revise your past and command your present thought. You can be a weed in the garden of your existence or a flower.

Yesterday is Today's Future

What was that again? That seems impossible. Yet Neville in his brilliance clarifies: "Yesterday is today's future. You may think it's past, but, by the curvature of time, you will discover it is not. When you begin to awaken you will come upon yesteryear in your future, and if you don't change it you will simply find yourself repeating it over and over, thinking you are doing it for the first time. But I ask you to awake that we may all enter this brotherhood of awakened humanity."

What does this mean? It means that the thoughts you send into the cosmos in your past are coming to fruition today, shaping and molding the life you experience even as you read these pages. They are the birds of your consciousness coming home to roost, and the circumstances you experience at this moment are the fruit of those seeds you planted yesterday. What you said "yes" to yesterday becomes your future, folding time back upon itself in a spiritual approximation of Einstein's description of space-time. The past becomes your future, and you live the consequences of past decisions and attitudes.

Clearly, you can see how transforming the mental experience of your days just done is vital for bringing about a different future. You cannot go back and alter the physical outcome of past days; if you lost a job or cheated on your lover, that's done. But you can alter the conscious reality of those days and change the experience where it is most real, in the mind. In fact, you must do this! You must change the tracks of your life or you will walk them indefinitely! Like Bill Murray in the movie *Groundhog Day,* until you change the fundamental nature of how you think about the world and humanity, you are doomed to repeat the same events and outcomes all your life. Your destiny was pre-set by your own thoughts long ago, but you can change it for the better by making conscious changes in your thought and action. Your life is like a worn track in the desert; if you remain on it, you are condemned to end up nowhere. To escape this fate, you must brave the unknown and create a new path.

> *You must change the tracks of your life or you will walk them indefinitely!*
>
> ༄ ༄ ༄

Change Your Past, Change Your Life

The self-help mavens of our culture spend a great deal of time talking about changing your future, but they clearly do not grasp the time-symmetrical nature of the Law of Revision, nor do they see that in order to transform your future, you must first transform your past. Neville, as he often does, articulates the need beautifully: "Changing your life means changing the past. The causes of any present evil are the unrevised scenes of the past. The past and the present form the whole structure of man; they are carrying all of its contents with it. Any alteration of content will result in an alteration in the present and future."

You can reach back into time and using the principles of Mind as reality, change the unedited thoughts of your past. Before reading this book and absorbing its teachings, did you have destructive thought patterns or mental images of want and need that brought you nothing but more want and need? It's likely that you did; most of us do. But rather than live with the present consequences of those thought patterns, God's Laws allow you to actually cast your mind back in time (and what is time but an illusion, as recent discoveries in physics have shown us) and edit past thoughts that were counterproductive. Those thoughts are the seed of any present evil or chaos in your life.

In order to move ahead with your life and take your place in God's System, you must go back and undo your disempowering thoughts and mental experiences. Until you do, the reality those thoughts have wrought, which is the reality you are experiencing right now, will continue to burden you. Only by revising the past can you prepare yourself for a brighter future. Follow this process in making this happen:

1. Find a quiet, meditative space where you will not be disturbed.

2. Rest and relax. Breathe deeply. Feel your body and mind come to a place of peace yet awareness.

3. Cast your mind back into the folds of time to periods when you know you had thoughts or made decisions that derailed your dreams or set you on a path that has proven to be unhappy.

4. Re-imagine those thoughts or choices in a new way. See the new consequences in your mind and make them real in your mental experience.

5. Repeat this as often as possible until the new outcomes become as real as your past physical experience.

Following this process will help you "dream things true." As you know, as the mind goes so follows the material reality. We live not in a *materialist monist* universe, where the only things that exist are elementary particles without consciousness or purpose, but in an *idealist* universe, where Mind is the fundamental substrate of all things. The idea is everything. By living a controlled, waking dream you change your past and bring the results of that changed past into your present in the form of greater fortune and deeper joy.

The Ultimate Creed

Revision or re-imagining your past creates a new reality in your present, one that redeems your past actions and choices. Otherwise, your past would be unforgivable. Not by God, because God forgives all things, but it's not God's job to forgive you for your own transgressions. That is your responsibility. But nothing is so bad that it cannot be imagined differently, and by doing so you can redeem yourself for past actions that would otherwise blight not only your life but the lives of others.

So redemption turns out, as does so much else, to be in our hands, not in the hands of the Lord. This turns so much of what we have been told is of Christian dogma upside down, but that is often what enlightenment requires: the courage to challenge one's own beliefs and listen to one's own guidance instead of taking commands from a creed laid down by another. I will tell you: the only authoritative creed you should have in your heart is the creed that you lay down for yourself, based on your enlightened vision for your life. Know and obey God's Laws as the vital underpinning for your reality, but as far as your Commandments, take them from your own mind and heart and goals for your life, not from some centuries-old dogma.

Keep your creed holy and keep it open to revision, because it will guide you into new paths and new revelations about your life and your Spirit. As Eric Butterworth writes, "The only compelling form of worship will be that to which a person's whole being responds instinctively and spontaneously; and the only church to which he or she will give allegiance will be the church to whose spiritual life and message he or she is irresistibly drawn."

Keep your creed holy and keep it open to revision...

So with this symmetry of time and causality, it should be clear to you now that in order to create the unified, joyous, fulfilled vision of your existence and purpose is to think from the end and work backwards. How must you change your consciousness today, given that today will become yesterday as time marches forward? Look at the end result you desire, such as wealth, a fine home, satisfying relationships or excellent health and determine what you must shape in your mental experience in order to set the wheels that will bring those outcomes turning. When you gain the insight to look both ahead and backward in time, you will gain greater power over your life and your future.

13

— THE LAW OF RETRIBUTION —

⌃ ⌃ ⌃

Retribution often means that we eventually do to ourselves what we have done unto others."

—Eric Hoffer

The word retribution brings to mind a host of provocative ideas. The most common of these ideas will be that of vengeance, which is the act of writing a wrong or enacting cosmic justice – or at least what we feel, in our limited human understanding, to be cosmic justice. However, that is not the meaning of retribution in the context of God's economy and the Laws of Being. Instead the long-standing concept of divine retribution, which has been held as so fearful by Christians for so many generations, it is inverted and becomes instead a law of divine love.

Under this new reality, retribution becomes not the stuff of vengeance but of fair return a love and faith one inputs into God's economic system. If the essence of retribution is "an eye for an eye," then it follows logically that what one streams into the psycho-reactive ether will be returned in kind. Therefore love permits us to do the right thing, to bring good upon ourselves and others by making ourselves prosperous and happy and developing this prosperity from the inside out. We caused no harm by being happy; in fact we make the world a better place of freer flowing divine Energy when we shed our impoverished nature and bring forth wealth and prosperity from the inside out, which is its only true source.

The mind creates reality, and so reality is subject to the energy of change that can either create or destroy.

೧ ೧ ೧

This becomes possible because the world you see through human eyes is only temporary. The true world is a spiritual one given its "psychogenesis" through world consciousness. The mind creates reality, and so reality is subject to the energy of change that can either create or destroy. In this sense the world is vulnerable to the thoughts of all, as all individuals have the power to bring their thoughts into manifestation. This is the "destroyer" aspect of divinity as described by John Randolph Price. With this reality, terrorism becomes a disease of world consciousness one that we create when we objectify a sick world consciousness focused on violence and division.

The Importance of Separate Identity

This is why whoever controls the images that permeate a society controls the destiny of its people. Images control and manipulate thoughts, which are the stuff of consciousness and therefore catalyst for our psycho-active reality. That is why African-Americans need to own their own media, so that we can control portrayal of African-Americans and therefore how all others think of us as well as how we think of ourselves. It is very easy to get caught in the illusion created by Hollywood that all African Americans are criminals, gang members and basketball players. Clearly that is not the case.

Many decades ago, before the civil rights movement, many educated successful blacks created their own segregated society. We created black colleges, black businesses, black newspapers, and an entire parallel society where we had control, we owned the property, and we moved our own people forward. It was a time of great achievement because we had the means to shape our own consciousness and therefore we had no limitations on what we could achieve. With integration into white society, which was justifiably seen as a victory, in many ways African Americans lost much of what we had gained. We lost our sense of separate identity, we lost much of our sense of self worth, and we lost our racial consciousness in trying to locate and behave like white society. When we should have fought for was desegregation, which would have given African-Americans access to those institutions of white society that we chose to be part of, while allowing us to retain our separate identity.

As the Rev. Al Sharpton pointed out, African-American Hollywood stars who have tried to become "more white" seem to have all become involved in scandals. It's as if after the American consciousness has mutated into something unrecognizable in which we don't love our own people for who when what we are. Such self-hating consciousness is a disease that afflicts every African-American no matter how successful.

The Lessons of Suffering

In our "scientistic" society (meaning a society where the presumed absolute knowledge of science has become as much a religion as any closed-minded fundamentalist faith), many atheists will use the existence of suffering as an argument for the non-existence of God. If God exists, they say, why does He permit such horrible atrocities to occur in the world? Why do children starve in Darfur? Why are children molested by their step-parents? But these questions show an ignorance of the true nature of God and Spirit. God is not a genie who grants every wish and aims to make the world a perfect place. He is a teacher and a guide and a Source of energy and inspiration. We do the work ourselves, and we create Hell or Heaven on earth. We're responsible.

Suffering, in this open-eyed cosmos, has a purpose. It is what Emmet Fox called a "benign and reformative consequence." Now, this is not true of all suffering. Some suffering, such as the horrific Christmas Eve Indian Ocean tsunami of 2004, does not fit into this description easily. Such events are simply tragedies that occur because the universe is a dynamic place where violence happens by chance sometimes. However, individual suffering of nearly any type is a lesson waiting to happen. Truly, you cannot control what happens to you in your life. However, you can control how you respond to what happens! You can choose to make suffering into an opportunity to learn and grow and send your life vectoring in a new direction. Or you can choose to wallow in self-pity and blame, as many people do.

However, you can control how you respond to what happens!

We all suffer because we have lessons to learn. A child gets burned when he touches a hot stove so that he will not play with matches when he's older. A small red place on his hand is better than him in the burn ward, packed in ice, with third-degree burns over 70% of his body.

Disease follows the same dynamic; it is telling you that something is out of balance in your body or mind, and that you'd better change it. Human beings need suffering to wake us up to the need for change, because we're remarkably self-deluding and shortsighted. For instance, diabetes and stroke affect a disproportionate share of blacks, and it's partially due to the "traditional" black foods many of us eat. Pig's feet, oxtail, chitlins... these were all unwanted scraps given to slaves, and they're very unhealthy. Yet we choose to eat them anyway, ignoring the effects on our health. We get obese and develop high blood pressure, and wonder why we're sick. Sickness is a messenger, not a punishment. It's God's way of reminding us: "You need to make wise choices, because I'm not going to bail you out."

There's No Escape

The Law of Retribution is impersonal and unchanging. It's not like the laws of men, which can be revised as the times change. It's a fundamental property of reality, so there is no escape from its effects. Your actions will always yield consequences according to their nature. You will reap joy or sorrow according to the decisions to make and the way you project yourself into the lives of others. This is why it is so important to treat other people with justice, compassion and love. Yes, it important to do those things for their own sake, but also because how the universe treats you will be affected by how you treat the people you encounter. What comes around truly goes around. This is the origin of the concept of karma.

The punishment for any act comes from the act itself. In the same vein, forgiveness of others confers upon us God's eternal forgiveness, as described by Ernest Holmes. As Jesus said, forgive and you will be forgiven. What we deliver into the fabric of reality will be delivered unto us in equal measure, for good or ill. Why do you think most criminals are caught? Because their acts sabotage them, no matter how smart they think they are. The act of causing chaos and harm or cheating another human being brings about an automatic cascade of misfortune in the life of he who commits a crime, and this misfortune always results in the person being apprehended and paying for his crime.

Emerson stated it beautifully in his *Essays*: "Every act rewards itself, or in other words integrates itself, in a twofold manner: first in the thing, or in real nature; and secondly in the circumstance, or in apparent nature." Everything you do brings its own rewards upon itself, even if you can't see the rewards develop for some time. Remember, much of what shapes your life is invisible: time, light, DNA. Just because you cannot perceive the consequences of your decisions does not mean they are not taking shape out of the range of your senses!

This fact brings the machinery of prosperity into clear focus for us. Good fortune comes about by two means: by deliberate act and by random circumstance of someone else's decision and action. To create the life you desire, do not wait for circumstance, for someone else to choose to act, for this takes your control of your own destiny out of your hands. Rather, take deliberate action with the reward in mind. Don't worry that you can't see the reward 24 hours later; take the action that you know brings good and health and peace and joy to others, because eventually, sooner or later, that action will bring those same results to you.

Rather, take deliberate action with the reward in mind.

☉ ☉ ☉

Emerson also wrote, "Men call the circumstance the retribution. The casual retribution is in the thing and is seen by the soul. The retribution in the circumstance is seen by the understanding; it is inseparable from the thing, but is often spread over a long time and so does not become distinct until after many years. The specific stripes may follow late after the offence, but they follow because they accompany it." What does this mean? That things happen on two levels: the physical and the spiritual. When you commit any act, you will see the physical rewards first in your consciousness. For example, if you lend money to a friend so he can start a business, he may pay you back with interest in a year. That is your physical result. But the spiritual result that resonates in your consciousness may not come for five years, and when it appears, it will be as good fortune that may have nothing (on the surface) to do with your friend's business. But if you understand how the Laws work, you will see the pattern.

Life is about patterns. When your doctor wants to get an idea of what your health risks might be, he asks how your parents and grandparents died. See the patterns and you'll see the consequences of your choices.

Life is about patterns ◌ ◌ ◌

Good Trumps Evil

Despite your best efforts, your life will be beset with challenges. If you're not dealing with a health problem, a marriage breakdown, a family crisis or financial turmoil right now, guess what? It's coming! The dynamics of causality are so complex and interwoven with intention and actions that only God understands them in their wholeness. So actions that you have forgotten may rebound upon you next month to bring misfortune into your experience, while the actions of someone you have never met may reverberate into your life in ways that bring bad luck and trouble.

But when bad things happen, you must not dodge them. That is unwise. Remember, the dark periods in life are inevitable consequences of living in a causal universe where we have free will; they are lessons clothed as trials, designed to bring you wisdom—if you choose to see it. So how do you deal with evil? How do you respond to it? You embrace it as something that must be processed by your Spirit and overcome by you becoming stronger, wiser, more resilient, or thinking in a new manner. The more you gyrate to avoid evil times, the more you deny their lessons and their power to spark your growth.

For example, if a woman in a terrible marriage ignores her pain and feelings of inferiority as well as her husband's infidelity because she does not want to face the pain and humiliation of divorce, then she may spend the rest of her life in a loveless relationship, constantly feeling small and violated. But if she embraces the pain and the evil times and ends the marriage, she deals with short-term agony but in the long term gains strength and power and self-awareness and new possibility. Her good trumps temporary evil in the end.

There is no scorn, anger or contempt in nature.

☽ ☽ ☽

One thing to remember is that the Law of Retribution is never vindictive. There is no scorn, anger or contempt in nature. It's not personal. There is simply no choice in the matter: when you commit an act in the experience of another, that act will come back to you. Nature gives you back what you sow. When you are uncomfortable and frightened, you exist in a different state of perception. Comfort falls away from your mind like discarded clothing and you "see" with new eyes. You see with Spirit, with Divine perception. In this way, you can see the imbalances inherent in your life and how to bring things back into balance.

Minding the Father's Store

Jesus said, "I must be about my Father's business." We are all minders of the Father's store, carrying out God's business in the plane of physical reality. Remember, you are flesh because God is pure Spirit; He needs each human being to carry out one tiny splinter of His great intention for the physical cosmos. It is your job to bring your own vision and energy to bear to bring your version of God's plan into existence and make it bear fruit.

Remember, you are flesh because God is pure Spirit;
☾ ☾ ☾

This is why the Law of Retribution exists: as a sort of "safety reminder" that when you give your appetites and passions to the venal, base and small in this world, you will be rewarded with meagerness and want. Many people spend their lives chasing sensation—sexual sensation, the lying sensations of drug use or drinking, the wild pleasures of gambling, crime or risk. Those create dopamine cascades in your brain that deliver temporary pleasure, but they are purely physical and therefore base and mean. They are distractions from your purpose, and if you devote yourself to them, you will reap the same superficiality from your life in return.

Instead, devote your appetites and passions to God and focus on your true nature, your spiritual nature. That is the definite, detailed covenant that you signed with God upon your birth—that you would serve as his faithful co-creator in your small corner of the universe! Amen! Focus your attention and intention on the spiritual and on bringing great joys, health and prosperity for others into manifestation and you will see the same in your life. Spirit makes it so, and is far mightier than the physical.

Phineas Parkhurst Quimby wrote in 1988, "All religion that embraces creeds is of this world and is governed by laws and contains rewards and punishments; therefore holding out inducements to be good with one hand and retribution with the other is not the religion of Christ." The religions of this world are created by *man*, not God. They are human institutions and subject to the biases and hidden purposes of their creators. When they talk of punishment for not adhering to dogma, that is punishment as conceived by man as a way to control the actions of others. It has nothing whatsoever to do with Christ.

> *The religions of this world are created by man, not God.*
>
> ☾ ☾ ☾

There is no condemnation for followers of Christ or servants of the Father. You are free to determine your own rewards! You do not need an intermediary telling you what is in God's Mind; you can discover that for yourself. You would not need this book or my teachings except that we all need guidance and reminders that this alluring physical world that we're so concerned with day to day is NOT the real world. Teaching, not dogma, is the path to God and to cosmic fruitfulness and plenty in your personal economy.

Retribution is Always Just

Ernest Holmes, one of the boldest and most courageous thinkers of the modern age of faith, broke new ground when he wrote, "I do not believe in hell, devil or damnation, in any future state of punishment, or any of the strange ideas which have been conceived in the minds of morbid people. God does not punish people... It is one thing to believe in hell and damnation and quite another proposition to believe in a law of just retribution." Holmes knew that the idea of eternal punishment and Hell is another human creation, just as more recently, the exiled bishop Carlton D. Pearson has written in his book, *The Gospel of Inclusion*. Jesus has said that the Devil is a liar, therefore, the Devil is a lie!

Heresy? Of course. But heresy is not a sin. It's an awakening. No human policy can or should stand between you and the fundamental truths of God. And that truth is that God does not punish. God does not NEED to punish; that is why he created Laws that would make our own natures self-fulfilling. The Law of Retribution always delivers just return for our actions. We punish ourselves for the evil that do by setting in motion and irrevocable flow of negative consequences that will come later in our lives. There is no punishment that we do not deserve, and no reward that we have not earned.

Now, Bishop, wait a second, I hear you say. Are you telling me that children who get brain tumors are reaping the punishment for some evil act? No, that's not what I'm telling you. God is not cruel. Some things happen by chance. The laws of nature and biology are not suspended because of the laws of spirit; they operate in parallel and must accommodate one another. Sometimes, bad things happen to good people. Sometimes children die. Sometimes good communities get leveled by tornadoes. Chance is a factor in human life, and God is not controlling the fall of every sparrow; that's not His task. Reward and punishment come into play when you are capable of making conscious choices— when you are old enough and self-aware enough to see a fork in the road and say, "Hmm, the left path will take me to the crack house and that prostitute at the pool hall, and the right will take me to church and my wife and volunteering to help the homeless." And you make a free choice.

When you reach a point in your life where you have the awareness to understand your choices and the foresight (which is a gift of God) to see the likely outcomes of your possible paths, you will begin to see retribution for good or ill. Children are not at that point, and communities are not punished for collective acts; God's laws are for the individual, not the collective. Sometimes, bad things just happen, and again, how you respond is everything.

Why Not a Little More Heresy?

We've come this far, so let's inch our way a little farther out on the cliff of dangerous faith. I'll say this: there is no evil. There is only energy in motion. The Law of Retribution is energy in motion, and when it brings the preordained results of your past actions into your conscious awareness, you interpret those results as good or evil according to whether they benefit or harm you. That's the nature of the universe in a nutshell: it's all about perspective.

There is no crime and punishment in God's system of cause and effect. We may think of God as the cosmic judge, but He has better things to do. That's why He created His Laws. They do the job automatically, and it is our task to learn about their nature and use it to bring order, peace, health and joy to this world. The good or evil you experience as a result of your choices and actions is merely the consequence of the energy you have set in motion. In the eyes of God, it is neutral.

So life is an effect and mind is the cause. Your thoughts set the energy of retribution in motion and bring about effects in your future experience, drawing them from the psycho-reactive stuff of the etheric plane. So when you change your thoughts, you set new energies in motion. This is why self-improvement is such a powerful path to walk. When you confront past patterns of failure or harm, accept responsibility for them and shift your personal paradigm, you are moving mighty forces of Mind to change the energy flowing into your life. You could still interpret the new results of this change as evil if you chose to, but who among us would interpret good health, a happy marriage and money in the bank as evil? The point is, it's all your choice. It's all you! You only need your enlightened self with a spiritual link to God's wisdom to remake your earthly experience in every way... and to bring about transformation in the lives of others around you.

We are, each of us, a well and a fountain. We carry deep water in our souls, deep water of power and thought that drinks of the wisdom of God's ancient creation. We are also a fountain that spills forth the water of life and healing to be drunk by others. Our blessings dwell deep within ourselves, to be regarded only by our innermost beings, and at the same time they gush to rain on others. We are all singular and all a multitude at the same time. We all owe each other everything, yet everything begins with each individual.

No East, No West

Many so-called religious scholars reject the idea of retribution because it smacks of the Eastern concept of karma, something that many Christians see as blasphemous. But as Emmet Fox writes, "Some Christian people, upon hearing the Law of Retribution explained, have objected that this is Buddhism or Hinduism, and not Christianity. Now it is perfectly true that this law is taught by the Buddhists, and by the Hinduists, and wisely so-because it is the law of nature. It is also true that the law is better understood in Oriental countries than among us; but this does not make it an Oriental possession. It simply means that the orthodox Christian churches have largely neglected to make an important section of the Christian teaching clear to the people."

There is no eastern wisdom or western wisdom. There is only wisdom and Truth, and the truths of God are the truths of nature, not the vain truths of someone's brand of religious belief, wrapped and packaged in a denominational name and endorsed by a convention or a pontiff. Truth is truth regardless of who states it. Retribution is a force of nature, part of the Tao of the earth, an aspect of the eternal harmony and flow of the universe: all things in balance, all things equal and coming around in like quantities in the end.

> *There is no eastern wisdom or western wisdom.*
>
> ☾ ☾ ☾

Neither East or West, the Tao of retribution is all about *flow*; all forces flow, from electromagnetism to gravity to blood to money. When flow and circulation are good, the body is healthy and the economy benefits everyone. When flow is restricted, things go sour. An example is a marriage in which one partner is always working to grow the relationship to new areas of communication, giving and love, while the other partner does nothing. That is uneven flow and it cannot be sustained. So, too, when you have an economy where the rich get all the benefit and the middle class is denied, eventually that economy will collapse, as we are seeing in our country now. This is why some medication does more harm than good; in treating symptoms of a disease rather than the disease, it interrupts the natural flow of the body.

This is all about wisdom, the wisdom to awaken to the future and see that it is shaped by what you do today. Jesus does not damn or condemn; He invites. He knows that your future is your *choice*. Each day represents a new opportunity to remake your mind and thoughts, to bring about new rewards from the Law of Retribution.

Act With Integrity

God has given us the means to govern ourselves. This is extraordinary. Free will is a gift beyond price. God could have chosen to make us His puppets, but He did not. He has granted us His power: to make and remake our reality. But we must do so with integrity. When we use the power of our minds (and even science is recognizing that the mind exists as a separate entity from everything else in the universe, with the power to reach out and heal and shape the material world) to coerce someone or force them to do something they would not normally do, we compromise our integrity.

As Joel Goldsmith writes, God governs the cosmos with infinite patience and wisdom, but He does so via His laws. The Laws will always deliver their ordained results according to God's timeless wisdom. But He expects us, having been gifted with the freedom and power to shape our reality, to act with the same wisdom and patience. We are reflections of the Divine Mind of God, and so we are charged with acting with integrity. This is your Divine inheritance. It is not something you need to attain, but it is a legacy you must grow into and discover how to use. You can use your power to plant seeds of hope and joy in the lives of others, or you can sow weeds to choke the lives of those around you. Know that whatever you choose, your garden will grow the same crop.

14

— THE LAW OF RELAXATION —

999

Your mind will answer most questions if you learn to relax and wait for the answer.

—*William S. Burroughs*

In Matthew 11:28, we read, "Come unto me all ye that labour and are heavy laden, and I will give you rest." Relaxation is underappreciated in our work-obsessed world. We all work long hours and spend much of our time trying to "force" good to happen for us. But if we've learned anything in our studies together of the Laws of Being, it's that the Laws are inevitable. We cannot force them to take effect. They come into play based on our actions, and their effects are irrevocable and universal. So the best thing we can do sometimes is relax, let our minds rest and dwell on the nature of Spirit and our relationship with the Divine, and let the Laws do their work.

The Law of Relaxation says that part of the way we bring God's forces of prosperity into effect in our lives is to "be still and know," letting our prayers flow freely into the cosmos without trying to force anything. When we let our minds come to God in their own good time, God comes to us. God meets Himself in us, and that can only happen when we are quiet of mind, meditative and open to hearing His voice. In those periods, when we release our prayers spoken in faith like doves into the fabric of spiritual reality, they bring about miracles.

Stop Contradicting Your Nature

As Catherine Ponder writes, "The prayer of relaxation has definite effects upon the body too. Tests show that up to 75 percent of the pain which exists when a person is tense and jittery vanishes when he relaxes."

The nature of disease is "dis-ease," the body's being ill at ease with the mind. Relaxation often cures this by allowing the body and mind to fall into the natural rhythms dictated by the universe.

Relaxation allows you to accept yourself completely

Relaxation allows you to accept yourself completely—your whole self, perfect and Divine in nature, without the contradictions of society, which can make you feel as though you are more flawed than you could ever be. This state of mind allows you to relax and love the truth of yourself, and to see that truth without blinders or self-delusion. This can be jarring and unnerving, as it involves letting go of the persona that you have created to fit into society and becoming You without artifice, the real You.

Letting go of the artificial self and developing mindfulness about who you really are without the context of social structures, money, or consumer culture is at the heart of all great wisdom traditions. This is the key to conscious, true living and the development of Divine consciousness. You will find this non-thinking, pure consciousness state of being in meditation, massage, acupuncture, yoga, and relaxation techniques that promote self-healing, such as visualization. These disciplines are an organized system of self-sanctuary, in which you discover the peaceful space within yourself and allow your mind to dwell there when you feel stressed out.

Eventually, over time, your mind dwells in that space more often until you become a permanent resident. This helps to prevent disease and stress, and gives you the equilibrium to deal with life's travails in a balanced, harmonious way. You must teach yourself to find the silent space within your mind.

Relieving the Pressure

From golf to music, masters of any discipline will tell you the same thing: relax and let it come. When you try to force results, results never manifest. So it is with the Laws of Being. You cannot force prosperity or good fortune to come into your life; doing so can actually drive it away with stressful, tense thinking. Mental pressure that we put on ourselves by feeling we must meet some set of cultural expectations for fitness, wealth and fashion, blocks creativity and harms our mental and physical well-being. Defusing that pressure is critical to fully realizing God's blessings.

You cannot force prosperity or good fortune to come into your life;

You cannot create something under force, because the effort defeats itself. The act of trying to force something to come into being blocks the flow of energy. You must center yourself first, know that your mind is the creative force that brings things into being, and allow the energy to come through you, not be manipulated by you. This is the spiritual world we're talking about, not the physical world. In the physical world, if you hit a nail harder with a hammer, it goes in faster. In the realm of the spiritual, the opposite is true! You need to relax and meditate and reach your silent center to allow good to flood into your consciousness.

The key to defusing the pressure to "make" things occur is prayer. Prayer is indeed a form of meditation that allows you to release your problems so the universe can bring forth solutions. Catherine Ponder writes, "The word 'relax' means 'to loosen' and 'to release.' When you practice the prayer of relaxation, you learn how to 'loosen' and 'release' your problems, so that they can be resolved." So peaceful meditation and prayerful relaxation are just as important as right mental activity in bringing health and wealth into your experience. The stress of today is just wear and tear on your mind; God wants you to dwell on things that are lovely and peaceful, to bring your mind to a place of weightlessness so that He can speak through it. Wise thought and wise relaxation are the opposite poles of creation that form the perfect whole. When the mind is staid and at peace, you will see results.

Divine Perfection

Repeat this mantra from the writings of Ernest Holmes:

"I am a center of Divine Perfection within me. I am free from every sense of burden, strain, or tension. My pulsation is in harmony with the Infinite Rhythm of the Universe. I am not troubled or concerned over the future, worried over the past, or afraid of the present. Perfect Love casts out all fear. The rhythm of my action is in perfect relaxation; its vitality is complete. The walls of my being are whole."

This should become a daily practice along with a prayer of relaxation. Find a sacred space in your home, a place where you can be undisturbed and the concerns of the material world cannot intrude on your mind. Then repeat these words and shape your awareness of Self— your knowledge of your being and your state of mind, connected with the cosmos. This is not idle thinking. The new integral science that is slowly transforming our materialistic culture is finding that all things are indeed interwoven and entangled. All minds and all matter affect each other and reach out to change each other's energy, so no one and nothing is isolated. We are each of us a multitude. Have this awareness within your Spirit and be still, and you will experience perfect love.

We are each of us a multitude.

You can see that relaxation is a conscious act. This is why monks and other master meditators spend decades learning to quiet the contentious, argumentative conscious mind and become pure being, pure non-thinking mindful consciousness. Relaxation must become something you do with deliberation and planning, every day, just as you might go to your gym to exercise. You must consciously still your soul and enter into the peace and silence of God's Mind.

Remember the twenty-third Psalm? It says that God "maketh me to lie down beside *still* waters." Stillness is the natural state of God's communication. In silence and stillness, your Spirit reaches out to God. Emergencies do nothing to move God's will; His Laws do not respond to need. Knowing God is within you and that your "I Am" can move mountains and shape the energies of the universe is what gets God to move through His Laws. Being still and contemplative readies the temple of God, your mind, to receive His blessings. The Laws bring them to you without fail.

Revelation in the Quiet

Burning bushes are rare. Booming voices from the sky don't happen daily. Don't be deceived by the idea that God needs to put on a special effects show to reach your mind and Spirit. He has no need. He's God. He can be subtle and quiet and overcome the "noise" of your mind and today's culture with its distractions. You won't find God in the noise, but in the stillness. As Vernon Howard wrote, "Relaxation attracts the answers." God revealed himself to the prophet in a still, small voice. Just like the eye of a hurricane is a region of unearthly calm, the Mind of God is defined by stillness and quiet. You can go out in the eye of a storm and not even realize anything is wrong, and the communication of God is this way. If you are not still and listening to the meaning of the calm, you will miss its power. Outside the eye, in the gyre of the storm is incredible power, but it is dwarfed by the power God carries in His quiet Spirit. In that calm is safety and peace.

And so your consciousness, properly shaped and wielded, can be your freedom. By choosing to let go of the pressure to achieve—to make things happen—that society places upon each of us with our tacit cooperation, you free yourself from stress and open your mind to the stillness in which you can hear God's voice. As Matthew 11:28 says, you are only as free as you are conscious of being. Or as Malinda Cramer writes, "Let your relaxation be complete, take no anxious care concerning yourself, use the truth you know and rely upon it, know that your consciousness of Truth is your freedom."

One Singular Sensation

The ultimate outcome of achieving perfect stillness in your mind is to discover the innate oneness that exists in all of us, but is masked by the noise of living. Deep meditation, mindfulness, finding that silent space in your consciousness—these are all ways to become one with yourself and one with life. This is the beginning of purpose and meaning, because when you strip away the distractions and discover your true self hidden at your silent core, you see who and what you really are. Your Divine nature becomes apparent, so obvious that you're stunned you missed it for so long. It becomes clear what you were intended to achieve.

Your purpose in life begins with yourself. Do not look to others for it. When you demand something of someone else, you lose command of yourself. Instead, achieve a state of full relaxation and you will achieve a state of full control over the potential of your life, because your Mind will be under your full command. Mind is the shaper of worlds, and so the peaceful, undistracted mind can bring anything into your reality. Eventually, relaxation becomes a permanent state, though like any discipline, this can take many years to realize. Start young! But with permanent relaxation comes the release of all the imaginary ideas we have about ourselves.

Your purpose in life begins with yourself.

Think about the mental baggage we carry from place to place in this life. Imaginary ideas about what we "must" do, "must" earn and "must" look like flood and burden our minds, pulling our attention and intention from the true nature of being. Relaxation is a path to releasing those imaginary self-imposed ideas. With them foremost in mind, as Vernon Howard writes, "A man cannot see how his self-pictures must always be at war with reality, causing endless tension and distress." Freed of them, we lose our tension and find our energy to create new possibilities.

Wise Relaxation and Wise Activity

We spoke earlier of wise relaxation and wise activity, the opposite poles of being. Properly balanced and attuned, they spark all events in life and bring a cascade of spiritual energy and potential into the mind. When I bring forth my prophecies, I do not "make" them occur. That's not something I can do; I am the conduit, not the creator. Instead, I reach a place of balance in myself. I "zone out" and become totally relaxed, getting to a place where I am not imposing my ideas or thoughts upon those of God. Instead, I become a vessel to be filled. That's the state of the Divine.

Look at DaVinci's fresco *The Last Supper.* The disciples are sitting in postures of relaxed attention; one even has his head on the Lord's breast. Ancient Greek culture is filled with the same depictions of men lounging around on porches and steps eating grapes and letting ideas come to them, forming the greatest civilization in human history. These men all knew that when you are in a relaxed state, knowledge flows.

How many times have you tried to "make" an idea come, only to end up blocked? Writers experience this frequently, and trying to struggle through writer's block only makes it worse. But when you quiet your mind and let your unconscious hum and putter along in the background, the Divine can speak without the overconfident chatter of your intellect to get in the way. Suddenly, inspiration strikes. You have the answer. That is how knowledge works; it comes when our minds are elsewhere and our true selves are open to its arrival.

You have the answer.

This is why it is so vital that you let go of those imaginary ideas about yourself and stop protecting your self-delusions. That version of your Self is the one influenced by others, by marketing and commercialism and religious dogma. But it is a lie! It is not who and what you are. Only by letting it go and embracing the real self can you relax and still your unquiet intellect to open to the constant flow of God's inspiration.

On Abundance

Again in the twenty-third Psalm, we read that "He maketh me to lie down in green pastures. He restoreth my soul." About this idea Holmes writes, "To lie down in a pasture suggests relaxation in the midst of abundance, an abundance which is already provided, a good which is Divinely given. The words green pastures refer to a place of rest. Green is the most restful and comforting color in nature. It brings to our minds the picture of a shady nook where we can rest in the middle of the day."

Green is the most relaxing, serene color there is. Dutch researchers have shown that people who exercise in the outdoors in a green, rural, natural setting get a greater benefit from exercise than people who do the same workout in a gym. Nature and green do indeed restore the soul. Relaxation is restorative; this is why when you get the flu, the first advice you're given is to go to bed and get a lot of rest. Why? Because your body has what it needs to fight off the infection... if you give it the chance. Rest restores our energetic balance, the yin and yang of our mind versus our body, that ancient tension that must be in harmony for us to be truly healthy. Without relaxation, we will know sickness without any real healing.

Abundance of health and wealth is the natural state of mankind, though we have forgotten the key to unlocking the vault of those wonders. The truth is that all God is, we are, and all we are, God is, at least in this world. We are God's proxies in the material realm, so He exists through us and our Minds as shaped by His inspiration and affected by His Laws. There is no future or past where God is not present. God is. Faith is knowing that God is, and as we know this truth and know that He is within us, relaxation comes naturally, as does abundance of healing, peace, knowledge and eventual reward.

Relax In the Cool of the Day

So your mission as a servant and surrogate of God is quite simple and wonderful: relax your mind and let God work through you. Be a vessel. Take time in the cool of the day—the serene part of the day when work is done and the world is quiet with the passing of light and shadow or the sound of rain—and hear His voice. Twice in the Bible (at least the King James version) is the world "cool" used: in the Garden of Eden and in the story of Lazarus. The voice of God walking in this world is always cool. God has no need for urgency or panic; He knows that these things bring no blessing.

Relax your mind and let God work through you.

Quiet and silence have immense power. Notice that God brought Eve out of Adam's silence. If Adam had been speaking, God would not have given him a helpmate. When you speak, God will not interrupt. Quieting your own voice allows God's cool voice to penetrate your mind and spread like the clear waters of a pristine lake, bringing peace and knowing. As Charles Fillmore writes, "The 'cool of the day' represents the relaxation or emptiness that follows sense expression. After the high tide of sensation has subsided, the voice of Jehovah God, commonly called conscience, is heard. Man is convinced that he has acted out of harmony with divine law."

The cool of the day. What a wonderful expression that evokes hushed, meditative silence in a harsh, loud world. Now you know that when you pray in the way prayer was meant—not as an asking for a specific favor from God but a deep, intense quieting of your intellect and an opening of your true self to the Infinite—you bring on relaxation of the most meaningful variety. You enter a state of consciousness known as *hypnogogic*, where your mind is almost at the state before falling asleep: hyper-aware but extremely calm and clear. This is the state when spiritual work can truly begin.

The Art of Prayer

So in the end, we see that prayer is an art form that takes years to master. It is not an intense form of asking for God to perform miracles like a genie from a bottle. Instead, prayer is a lifelong discipline no different from earning a black belt in a martial art. It is the act of placing your all-powerful Mind in a state where God can show you the path to bringing about your own miracles.

Prayer is the perfection of the God-given Mind,

Catherine Ponder writes, "The Oriental method of prayer teaches that relaxation and control of the body, cleansing of thought and emotions, deep breathing, followed by turning inward and practicing concentration, meditation and ecstatic union with one's divine self are all steps of prayer that must come first. Then only in the advanced phases of one's prayer development—after one has mastered all these phases— does one have the ability to manifest things or to immediately realize one's desires." Prayer is the perfection of the God-given Mind, our greatest gift and the seat of our Divinity and humanity.

Prayer is an illusion of sleep that blocks the sometimes baleful influence of that demanding, frenetic and materialistic outer world in which we must dwell. It is our secret garden gate to a world of relaxed consciousness where anything becomes possible, a parallel state in which the enlightened individual must exist in order to fully serve God. So relax. You have miracles within you. Discover your peace and silence and let God reveal them. Amen.

15

— THE LAW OF THE CHRIST MIND —

9 9 9

The Christ mind is the veil between the conscious mind and the inner worlds of God.

—*Sheila R. Vitale*

Now we come to another controversial issue: the nature of Christ. The meaning of "the Christ" in our modern age has been a subject of debate among theologians, and it remains so. The word comes from the Greek "khristos," meaning "the anointed." This title was given to Jesus of Nazareth in recognition of His place as God's anointed Son and the bearer of the message of redemption and compassion for all mankind. So the term Christ is not necessarily limited to the being, Jesus. It is a reference to anything that is anointed by God. So when we speak of the "Christ Mind," we are speaking of a consciousness anointed by God and bound up with the purpose of manifesting Divine intent. In essence, the Christ Mind is in all of us, in our potential. Creation is an inside job.

In Phillippians 2:5, Scripture reads, "Your attitude should be the same as that of Christ Jesus." In other words, the Divine Mind should reside in you as it did in Jesus, making you a co-creator with God. God resides in you, if you allow Him to. Everything begins with you, so when you follow the Christ mind within you and let it guide you to greatness, you will achieve wonders. Everything you desire has its root in your thought, then presses out your experience in this material reality. You should be able to look at the world and find it pregnant with good—pregnant with your own version of the Christ child, your own savior.

The Greatness of Your Spirit

During his 32 years dwelling on this earth as a human, Jesus was not interested in theology or religious politics. He did not manifest among us to start a religion; He did so in order to shape the human spirit, because being of God, He knew that the Spirit is the power source for all change on the material plane of reality. He knew that the God-mind was always trying to reach out and work its Will through the minds of men, so those minds needed to be shaped and made aware of their great place in the grand plan.

> *Jesus was not interested in theology or religious politics.*

The God/Christ mind thinks through you. You will know this when you are at peace and your consciousness makes leaps of awareness or intuition that seem to come out of nowhere. When those moments occur, that is your God-mind speaking. As Ernest Holmes made clear, our capacity to be great and loving is due to the greatness of the Spirit within us. Holmes and Raymond Charles Barker wrote, "There is an interior Christ-Mind that baffles all reasoning and is beyond all human explanation. In me at this moment, God abides in fullness, in richness, in omniscience. My life today is the life of God. My thinking this day is accomplished because the God-Mind thinks through me. My capacity to be a great and loving person is because greatness born of the Spirit indwells me."

The spirit within each of us is the wellspring of all our ideas, inspirations and flights of genius. The human mind is the conduit for the inspiration of Spirit, a memory bank receiving and storing the incoming communication of God to be turned into practical action and spiritual thought in this physical reality. Every thought you will ever need to solve problems in your world is already given to you by the Spirit dwelling within you, because that spirit maintains a constant open link to the Mind of God. If you are aware, you are never apart from God. This is why the only true Hell is a state of total isolation from God. Your mind is completely contained and nourished by the God/Christ Mind.

Be Still and Sense the Presence

Last chapter we discussed the importance of Relaxation, and the Law of the Christ Mind highlights why this is so. Only when we silence our conscious minds, the minds that think they have all the answers and are wiser than God, can we feel the Divinity that presses against our consciousness. Herein lies the great benefit and wisdom of meditation. True meditation quiets the sense of Self that underpins so much of our identity in this tangible reality. That Self is both our blessing and curse; it lies to us and tells us we are the Prime Movers of our lives, yet it is the effective tool that allows Spirit to achieve greatness in the world. Wisdom lies in learning when to give the Self—the ego—free rein and when to shut it down.

Stilling the noisy, arrogant Self creates a peaceful void into which the incarnation of God can enter your mind and speak to you. This is what we mean when we say you must become "born again" to truly experience God's love. This does not mean simply saying you accept Christ and then coming to church; plenty of people do those things without ever meaning them and without grasping the true nature of the Laws of Being. No, being "born again" means being able to suppress your egotistical Self and allow God to fill you. It means making room regularly for the Lord's Voice and Mind and Spirit in the temple of your mind. Consciousness is the temple of the Christ mind, and when you are fully in the Spirit, you will be able to consciously feel the Divine energy of the Christ mind flowing into you and allow it to work through you. This begins with meditation, but when you are advanced enough, you will be able to do it all the time, like breathing. This is the state of being of the prophets.

The Human Mind and the Christ Mind

Even though the human mind is a purpose-built conduit for channeling the Spirit of the God-mind, there are profound differences between the human mind and the Christ-mind. The human mind is fundamentally interested in itself, as reflected in how we tend to think. Reflect on your thoughts and you will see how often "I" and "me" thoughts fill your mind: my children, my job, my health, my money. That is human nature and it's something we strive to overcome in order to be proper servants of the God-mind.

The Christ mind is all about the welfare of others. "Love thy neighbor as thyself" and "pray for thine enemies" are typical thoughts of the Christ mind. This is a far more evolved consciousness, one that has taken shape over the eternal epoch of the cosmos. Our goal is to evolve in mind to become more like the Christ mind, reaching out with thought to shape the paths and fortunes of others. In the end, we must let egotism go. There is only one power in existence, and it is not Man. It is the spiritual power of God that shapes all ends. Only a person who has the unshakable conviction that all power flows from the Divine Mind has some measure of the Christ-mind, and even a tiny measure, a grain of that consciousness, can do wonders.

So though your human mind is flawed, you have within you the potential to become more like Christ—to transform your consciousness and plant the seed of the Christ-mind in yourself. This is done through affirmations, statements of profound wisdom which, when spoken aloud, actually bend the conscious mind and over time, change it as the wind eventually bends a tree into a new and sinuous shape. As Charles Fillmore has written, "Christian metaphysicians have discovered that man can greatly accelerate the growth in himself of the Christ Mind by using affirmations that identify him with the Christ. These affirmations often are so far beyond the present attainment of the novice as to seem ridiculous, but when it is understood that the statements are grouped about an ideal to be attained, they seem fair and reasonable."

Your mind alters as your ego dies.

Speaking daily affirmations to yourself—phrases such as "I am like Christ in my ability to think only of the peace and welfare of others," or "I partake of Christ's mind by opening my consciousness to the fullness of God's Divine thought"—brings about a wonderful transformation over time. Your mind alters as your ego dies. You become a clear vessel for God to fill with light.

Free of Error

In the Christ-mind, there is no error. There may be the misunderstanding of the limited human mind, but there is no errant thought or intent. Prayer reminds us of the potential genius within us and gives us the spark to find brilliant solutions to problems in our lives. When you are one with the Christ-mind, it will guide you to the right decision as a compass inevitably guides a well-navigated ship to a safe harbor. There can be no mistakes.

This is the case because when you share a mind with Christ, you become as He was: a vehicle for the flowing, infinite knowledge and Will of the Father. Jesus said that it was not He who worked miracles or moved the minds and hearts of men, but the will of His Father acting through Him. When God abides in your mind and Spirit, He moves your limbs and mind to accomplish whatever you wish. This cannot be any other way. Even in a higher state of consciousness, all knowledge and power of a world-shaping nature flows from God. Man can do nothing on his own.

Man can do nothing on his own.

ᖆ ᖆ ᖆ

So if God is speaking to and through our Christ-mind at all times, why don't we always hear Him? We do. What we don't always do is *listen*. Listening is an active process that involves humility, the willingness to admit that one does not know everything. Some humans are, to be charitable, lacking in this quality. One of the strongest human impulses is the desire to delude ourselves that we *know* the nature of reality; this is why science makes so many ironclad pronouncements about medicine, the cosmos and so on, only to say, "Whoops, did we say that? Um, we were wrong" a few years later. To truly listen to God and be in the state of the Christ-mind, we must admit what we do not know, and love the state of non-knowledge as a state of learning.

This is the real value in open consciousness and humility. Only then can we receive the fullness of the Christ-mind as it was when Jesus walked this earth. We open our minds to the inflow of teaching and enlightenment. Every day becomes a master class in kindness, wisdom and spiritual growth. We become part of the light of the world.

We Are One

So the unity of God and man, so often spoken of by cutting-edge theologians, is demonstrated by the Law of the Christ-mind. In becoming a free-flowing vessel for the Father's infinite Mind, we see the works that Mind can work upon the world through us. We see the results through our actions as what we touch and the words we say seem to have Divine power Doors open, spirits of others respond. It is truly astonishing and wonderful to perceive. The entire plane of physical beingness responds to the Voice of God, spoken and worked through you, as a flower does to the sun. It is the natural state of this God-created reality to respond to its Maker. With us and the Father in unity, anything becomes possible.

When you obey the Christ-mind, success follows.

999

When you obey the Christ-mind, success follows. That spirit is seeking a conduit always, and if it doesn't find one in you, it will find one in somebody else. Do you really want someone else to have that wondrous anointing but to be denied it yourself? The relationship as a prophet of God through the Christ-mind is a consummation devoutly to be wished. As Charles Fillmore so brilliantly wrote:

"Whoever seeks supply through Spirit and submits his cause to the law of justice and righteousness always succeeds. The reason why men fail

to demonstrate the many promises of divine support is that they cling to some selfish or unjust thought. Once the Christ Mind is perceived and obeyed, success follows. God prospers us when we give the best that is in us and do all things unto Him, acknowledging Him in all our affairs. This is a sure way to success, and when success does come we should realize that it resulted from the work of Spirit in us, because we made ourself a channel through which the Christ Mind could bring its ideas into manifestation."

Amen! In Job 36:11, Scripture says, "If they hear and serve Him, They will end their days in prosperity, and their years in pleasures." Serving God by allowing your mind to shed Self and ego and walking in the daylight as a receptacle for the Christ-mind brings personal reward and greatness upon you. There is a term in astrology called *progression*. Don't get nervous; astrology actually has a basis in Eastern Vedic science and is not counter to the reality of God. How could it be when God made the stars and planets?

In progression, the differing terms of your life correspond to one another and predict what your life will be like. For example, if you are 48 years old, look at the 48th day after your birth. What happened? You will have to ask your parents, if they are still alive, what happened in your home. But what happened in the world on that date? Was there war and tragedy? Or was there peace and hope? The events of that day will prophesy what your 48th year will be like. If the day was violent and tumultuous, you best batten down the hatches and gather your strength, because you will have a lot to endure.

Well, God pays attention to progression. He is in the business of giving a year for a day. Jesus ministered for three years and it was three years before He rose after the crucifixion. Pay attention to numerology:

there were 12 disciples, and $1 + 2 = 3$ days. The numbers in your life all have significance if you know how to make sense of them. This is where asking a prophet makes so much sense. How is God speaking to you through the numbers of your life?

The Christ-Mind is Eternal

We hear a lot about evil in this world and from mainstream Christianity. Man is supposed to be fundamentally evil, redeemed (and just barely) only through giving himself to Jesus. That is nonsense. God does not create anything that is evil. Even the Devil was and is not evil. Evil is a human concept. Instead, say that we are fundamentally tempted to follow paths that lead us to tune God out, to fail in our duty to become the Christ-mind.

> *God does not create anything that is evil.*
>
> ☉ ☉ ☉

But when we live in the Christ-mind, it automatically separates evil out like a spiritual centrifuge. Evil descends to that carnal place where it belongs and we are no longer tempted and guilty; we no longer have the desire to stray from God's Voice. Nothing is more joyous and more satisfying than knowing that we are fulfilling our destiny as a vessel of the Lord. No sex, money, food, drink, drugs or gambling can surpass that!

Fillmore writes, "Christ existed long before Jesus. It was the Christ Mind in Jesus that exclaimed, 'And now, Father, glorify thou me with thine own self with the glory which I had with thee before the world was.'" The Christ-mind existed long before Jesus. Jesus was a man in human flesh and blood, but a man who was completely and utterly dwelling in the Christ-mind. He was pure Christ-mind, without an ego or a vain Self to block the least of His Father's words. The

Christ existed in the Mind of God before time; it has no beginning or end. In this state, Christ was not Jesus; the man had not yet been born. Christ began as part of the Spirit of God, part of God's consciousness that was able to set aside the Self and open to the Voice within. Who does God pray to? To the universe, hearing the trillions of voices of evolving reality. That is the Christ-mind in God! Only when the man Jesus became manifest did Christ Jesus become a being. The Christ is eternal. Our Christ-mind is eternal.

That's huge stuff. Christ as thought, not man? God praying to something? Wow. Have I blown your mind yet? Well, your Christ-mind, when you discover it, knows these truths already. The Christ-mind is one with the Mind of God, and all power and knowledge in heaven and earth flows from it. So you have access to all knowledge, all enlightenment as you quest for spiritual perfection. Nothing begins within us; all is without, but it flows to us in limitless supply and love from God and flowers within us if we let it.

Your Task

We want to experience that oneness, that knowledge, that potential for change and joy. Of course we do! It is our nature coming back to us! To make it happen, however, you must rearrange your thoughts according to the Christ-mind: all things to your brothers, all things from God, nothing for or about that egotistical Self. Be like Christ as he was as Jesus and you will bring your mind into correspondence with God's perfect harmony. God wants this of you. He wants you to become His perfect servant, his co-equal creator of new and wonderful realities.

This demands mindfulness—the conscious awareness and control of one's thoughts. Our thoughts are like sheep, easily led astray and out of synch with God if we are not mindful. So it becomes a daily discipline for the prophets and other enlightened ones to stand back and regard our minds with what is known as *meta-cognition*, saying, "How am I thinking? Is my mind open to God's Voice? Am I thinking and feeling Christ-like thoughts?" This constant monitoring is essential to staying on track and being in harmony with God. No one is perfect; no one stays in synch all the time. But we can all strive to do better.

Being in the Christ-mind will make you a "mystical millionaire." This is the state in which riches flow in untold amounts into your consciousness: ideas, inventions, inspiration, direction. You have only to be open to them and to act on them with your consciousness and your hands will flow with gold. The biblical example is Melchizedek, to whom Abraham gave a fortune in tithes. He was the original spiritual millionaire, a symbol of the creative power of the Christ-mind and of the "I Am" within you.

> *As time passes, it will become clear that we are all eternally at one with the Christ-mind.*
>
> ☾ ☾ ☾

As time passes, it will become clear that we are all eternally at one with the Christ-mind. That is the meaning of the word *atonement*: at-one-ment. It means to be as one with the Source of our being and our creative power. When we dwell in the Christ-mind and walk in the waking world as open, loving beacons of that Divine thought, we need only turn our conscious human mind and "I Am" consciousness to what we want to achieve and we will see every righteous wish fulfilled. That is true, everlasting wealth in this world and the next.

As Joel Goldsmith writes, "Is it not clear then that man's at-one-ment with mind, being established in the beginning through the relationship forever existing between God and His idea, man, it requires no conscious effort to bring about or to maintain. The awareness of this truth is the connecting link with divine consciousness."

Amen.

16

— THE LAW OF PARALLELS —

꩜ ꩜ ꩜

"Both abundance and lack exist simultaneously in our lives, as parallel realities. It is always our conscious choice which secret garden we will tend...when we choose not to focus on what is missing from our lives but are grateful for the abundance that's present—love, health, family, friends, work, the joys of nature and personal pursuits that bring us pleasure—the wasteland of illusion falls away and we experience Heaven on earth."

—Sarah Ban Breathnach

The Law of Parallels says that when we parallel the life of Christ, we become one with God and gain power untold. Our power is magnified because of our godly nature, so one plus one does not equal, two but infinity. When you are tethered to God as a parallel being, your ability to effect change in the world jumps by orders of magnitude. On your own you might become 1,000 times more powerful. Add another parallel being, someone who shares your state of enlightenment, and you can square that number to one million times more potent. So you can see how adding more and more people with their "I Am" awareness fully in place can lead to near-omnipotence in this world!

There are more opportunities to join together than any time in history. Thanks to the Internet and other communications technology, thanks to the spiritual revival that's happening throughout the world, people are coming together in spiritual awareness as never before. This, the power of transmutation is raised to an unprecedented level. That is why ten giants can save a city: you are mighty in numbers, because when you mirror God, you also reflect one another. Ever see twin mirrors reflecting each other? The images regress into infinity. That is what happens when you become a mirror for God's intent.

This parallelism is God's design, and it is reflected in the Bible. In Exodus, God spoke to Moses as a friend. Not as a creation, a servant or a subject, but a friend! Moses was but a man, but God also saw that Moses was a higher being in his enlightenment and willingness to give his consciousness over entirely to God's purpose—to be God's vessel. Moses could be the vessel because he mirrored God in mind and understanding of the spiritual, psychological nature of the universe. God did the same later with Jesus, saying, "This is my son, in who I am well-pleased."

Jesus was incarnated as Man, but he was a perfect mirror for God. In essence, when you parallel God you empty yourself of everything else: ego, goals, fears, doubts. You become a clear crystal filled with Divine Light, as Christ was. Many times in the Bible, and especially in Isaiah, God talks about how He elevates His good servant and makes him His proxy and voice to the nations of the world. God wants to be proud of you, and He is most proud when you mirror Him—when you become Him.

Baptism and Seed

Matthew Fox writes, "Thus, a new creation story, a Cosmic Christ event, is alluded to in the baptism of Jesus when it was revealed to Jesus that he was a Cosmic Christ just as the transfiguration event is a revelation to others of Jesus' being a Cosmic Christ."

In the creation, things were set in motion that cannot be undone, and the greatest of these was the baptism of the world in the waters of the deep. Water takes whatever form it is given, much like Mind. So when God said, "Let there be..." and brought about manifestation, the things that came into being were baptized and given form in this cosmic initiation rite. So was it with you, given form from formlessness in your mother's womb, and when you pass out of this body you will be formless again, pure Consciousness ready to elevate to the next stage of existence. Creation took place at the beginning of time, but the act is repeated every moment of every day—every second is a new Genesis, with the manifestation baptized in the waters of Mind.

In this view, each idea you have has within it the seeds of new creation.

ᦙ ᦙ ᦙ

This "new creationism" takes creation from a hoary, ancient story tucked into the beginning of an old book and makes it fresh and new. In this view, each idea you have has within it the seeds of new creation. It will produce fruit according to the kind of psychological soil you plant it in, just as seeds in earth produce according to the soil nutrients, water, sunshine and beneficial insects. However, your seed will only produce what your character is able to plant. As Charles Fillmore writes, "A thistle seed will always produce thistles, regardless of the character of the soil; a low ideal will likewise work out low conditions in a high type of mind."

So every thought that finds refuge in your mind and gains credibility in your awareness will flower there, intentionally or unintentionally. The farmer does not crave weeds to grow in his fields, yet they come unbidden; so with us, thoughts of sickness or misfortune that gain a hold in our minds can and will grow such outcomes even if we do not consciously intend to bring such darkness down on our heads. The seeds will grow in the baptismal water of Mind as sure as the sun rises.

Walking With Jesus

It would seem to be nearly impossible to prevent stray thoughts of disease and disaster from entering our minds, so are we doomed to lives of random misfortune unless we can develop the discipline of monks? No. Again, the example of Jesus saves us. Christ existed on this earth not just as teacher and vessel for God but also as a model for us to parallel. That is why so many of Christianity's wisest teachers preach that to be a true Christian is not to follow any dogma, but to parallel Christ—to live in mind and spirit like Him. It is also why Gandhi famously remarked, "I like your Christ. I do not like your Christians. They are so unlike your Christ."

*Christ existed...
as a model
for us
to parallel.*

Mirroring the mindset of Jesus allows us to undergo a transfiguration, to become willing vessels of the Lord, to move forward and evolve. We are meant to do this; our brains contain "mirror neurons" that are designed to respond to the behavior of other people in a like way, which is why we enjoy being around positive individuals and why laughter is contagious. This structure of our brain, the most complex construct in the universe, allows us to self-model our thinking after the Source of our minds: God. When we parallel Jesus, we empty ourselves and give ourselves over to struggle and self-discovery, as He did. The travails that our mind plants for us—financial difficulties, health problems—become tests that help our souls mature, so that we can truly become mirrors of Christ.

Parallel spiritual states are seen in our traditions of atonement. Remember that the word breaks down to "at-one-ment," meaning that we are unifying with the Source of our mind and consciousness. In traditional atonement ceremonies, such as the Eucharist and the Jewish tradition of sacrifice, people would seek to placate God and receive forgiveness for their sins through surrender and sacrifice to God. But with our more enlightened sensibility, we know that God does not judge our actions. Our actions reward us through the Laws in exactly the way that we deserve. There is nothing to atone for. Rather, our true sacrifice comes when we surrender our egotistical Self in order to become a perfect vessel for God's Will. That is at-one-ment: giving up our illusion of separateness, becoming like Christ, in order to allow Divine energy to propel us toward our destiny.

Sacred Symbols

Once upon a time, mysticism was not so remote from daily life. We lived alongside the mystical daily, looking to shamans and sacred signs to cast light on the world we lived in during an era when the scientific method had not yet given us the tools to systematically investigate things and make new discoveries. You could say that spirit and intellect were out of balance, with intellect playing a minor role. In those days, sacred symbols were windows into our future and our individual destinies.

Because science has aggressively banished the mystical from our lives, spirit and intellect remain out of balance, only now intellect holds sway and many of us are diminished in our ability to perceive the metaphysical reality of things. But both spirit and intellect are gifts from God and equally vital; sacred symbols continue to hold great significance for us and our understanding. When you go for psychotherapy, your doctor asks about the people in your life—family, friends, pastors—because they are a looking glass in which you are reflected. We all have sacred symbols in our lives.

The windows in cathedrals were designed to allow the worshipper to look through them and seek revelation, because the stained glass cast the world in a new light, forcing a change in perspective and thought. The problem is, many of us have come to worship the window, not seek revelation. We don't want revelation; that would upset our comfortable, ignorant lives. We want positive messages of self-help and warm fuzziness, but that's not what God wants. He wants us to face the hard changes, to take the risks, to dare to step away from dogma and complacency and stand on the edge of revelatory truth. We need to be looking for symbols that will guide us on great quests of discovery: serpents in the wilderness, Jesus on the cross, harvest harbingers. We should always be on the lookout for symbols and signs that lead us down that path of revealing and prayer, because the signs are everywhere! We have just forgotten how to see them, but we can learn.

> *The problem is, many of us have come to worship the window, not seek revelation.*
>
> ☾ ☾ ☾

When we begin to notice the signs and symbols, we can pray from a place of knowing, not begging. Remember that God's economy does not respond to want or need ("Please send me some money, God"); it responds to the mental reality of achieved creation ("Thank you God for the money I have already received"). Symbols can remind us of the reality of our thoughts and serve as guideposts to the kind of manifesting prayer, turning it into an invocation that transforms thought into 3D reality that finds its way into our experience.

Separation Is Illusion

Hell is a state of separation from God that is self-caused; God will never separate Himself from you. Unless you choose to separate yourself, there is no separation; there is only parallel existence. That parallelism is actually God's push to reunify all of creation. There is a reason that He did not declare the second day of Creation; He needed to separate from the universe in order gain perspective on what He had created. Since that day, God has been trying to reunite all creation, and that marriage and wholeness happens in each of us individually. God cannot be separated from His creation any more than mind can be separated from body. In the end, we all come back to God.

This brings us into a discussion of physical and spiritual bodies and the nature of knowledge. You see, Heaven and Hell are not places; they are states of mind. Earth is the same way: it is an illusion masquerading as a place with limitations. It is not. This material world is a shell hiding a psychic, conscious reality in which Mind is the ultimate force for creation and destruction. This blend of the physical and the mental is what Rene Descartes called *duality*, that is, the reality of Mind being a separate entity from Body. Reductive science spent many years dismissing this idea, but new discoveries are showing us again that the Mind is a real force, the ground state of the cosmos.

> *Heaven and Hell are not places; they are states of mind.*
>
> ☉ ☉ ☉

Because of this, as philosopher Emanual Swedenborg wrote, human beings carry about a celestial connection to the terrestrial. As Holmes wrote, "There are bodies celestial and bodies terrestrial...so also is the resurrection of the dead...The body is sown in weakness, it is raised in power: it is sown a natural body, it is raised a spiritual body. For there is both a natural body and a spiritual body." We are all mystical in nature, seers of sacred symbols and weavers of psychic miracles. Plotnius, the king of the mystics, was a man like any other, not a cosmic being except in the sense that we are all cosmic beings. You must discover your own mystical side and begin to see the significances all around you, the patterns that are clues to the truly mystical, Mind-based nature of this reality. Look that what you already know: there are nine organ systems in the body (cardiovascular, pulmonary, nervous, endocrine, urinary, circulatory and so on), each corresponding to one of the nine cosmic patterns. There are seven sense organs on the face, and seven days in the term of Creation. There are hidden patterns everywhere!

There are hidden patterns everywhere!

Once you see the patterns you will begin to see God everywhere. He works in symbols and patterns because in making us work to discover His signs and communications, He trains us to become more spiritually aware and cognizant of our own higher nature.

Laws and Parallel Universes

In the same way, there are natural and spiritual laws that govern all the universe. The Laws we're discussing here are only some of them, though they are among the most important. For every natural law, there is a corresponding spiritual law. This is the Law of Parallels playing out again, shaping the order of things. Dr. Alexis Carrel said that faith, without violating any physical law, uses another set of laws that transcend physical laws. Faith is the mastery of spiritual laws, while living is the co-existence with natural laws over which you have no control. In the spiritual realm, you can do far more than be a spectator.

Science, which has become our dominant paradigm for explaining reality, has long struggled with the ideal of parallelism. Yet this idea is coming into the foreground with new studies into the nature quantum mechanics, the "mystical" side of physics. In the spiritual realm, we say that every dream, every idea, every alternate action is already present in a reality parallel to our own, which is why anything you need can be tapped into by simply breaking down the walls between parallel streams of causation. Well, now science is waking up to this idea.

In quantum mechanics, everything exists only as probability until a conscious mind observes it (which explains how the cosmos was able to evolve before humans existed to observe it; God was the Mind observing). When that observation happens, those infinite probabilities were thought to "collapse" into one reality. Now many physicists think that instead of collapsing each probability simply splits off into its own parallel reality. This means that every second, billions of parallel realities are being birthed out of the foam of the universe! This means infinite plenty and supply for us to access!

This means infinite plenty and supply for us to access!

ↃↃↃ

When Jesus fed the 5000 people in the Bible, He tapped into this limitless power source. He did not have the fishes and loaves in the physical realm to feed the multitude, but He knew that in a parallel universe the food existed. He simply opened His mind and gave thanks, and by doing so He allowed the spiritual, psychic energies to flow freely between worlds, and the food manifested. The Mind is the key to the door between parallel realities, and each of us is a gatekeeper.

Parallels can also be seen between body and mind. The literature of complementary and alternative medicine (CAM) is overflowing with incredible stories of the mind-body link: powerful results of the much-maligned placebo effect in which people have caused wounds or carvings to appear spontaneously on their skin, cases in which people with terminal cancer who practiced deep visualization meditation and saw their bodies destroying the cancer went into miraculous complete remission, intentionality studies in which thousands of individuals sending loving, healing intentions from another continent have effected measurable positive health results on sick patients, and many more. The more stubborn healthcare professionals and scientists do not want to acknowledge the reality of these effects; they smack too much of a Dark Ages mysticism that modern science has been eager to exorcise from our lives. But you can't exorcise what's real, and even more what helps people to heal and lead longer, better lives.

Everything is under one power and one mind.

ღ ღ ღ

Everything is under one power and one mind. You are a reflection of the Living God's Mind, so it is no wonder that your mind has such incredible control over your body. There are truly no wonders that the mind cannot achieve. Ideas generate energy, move men and women, produce money and prosperity, shape the world, and light lamps of hope and change. Every time you create a new idea in your mind, you are creating a thing, a force that flows into the psycho-reactive plane of reality and sets other forces in motion. As Fillmore so eloquently wrote, "Ideas generate energy with a swiftness unparalleled in physical dynamics. Rather than moving inanimate things, they move men and women. Rather than temporarily lighting our streets for a few hours, they light the lamps of intelligence that burn eternally."

The Laws of Nature and Thought

The Laws of nature and thought are identical; we are living in a universe where the physical serves the needs of the spiritual, which is ascendant. Throughout history there have been profound mystics who have recognized this, starting with Jesus and moving on to beings like Buddha, Plato, Socrates, Jung, Einstein, Swedenborg, Emerson and Whitman. These men saw clearly that beyond the comprehensible physical realms lies a spiritual realm that must be experienced to be understood; reality is a *subjective* state, one that does not reveal itself to observation and experiment. They taught the principles of parallel reality, and Jesus Himself taught His parables in order to illustrate the sameness of thought and nature.

> *...your Divine mind has to overcome your carnal mind to put these spiritual laws into action.*

This parallelism between thought and things is automatic and self-operative. The only catch: your Divine mind has to overcome your carnal mind to put these spiritual laws into action. As we have discussed many times, making the Laws work for you means surpassing your physical, limited, "what I see before me is all that is" nature and making thought, not labor, your currency of creation. Heaven and earth are parallels, so that what is occurring on earth is also happening in the infinite spiritual realms of Mind and Consciousness, and communicating itself in waves of mental energy that travel through the cosmos. Strife in one place breeds strife in all places, while peace and love bring about the same across the universe. The forces of nature bend to spiritual laws. Loving thought can pacify the earthquake and quiet the storm.

As Holmes writes, "The practitioner is not using Divine Mind to overcome a carnal mind. He is using a harmonious thought to overcome a discordant mental atmosphere. The basis of his work lies in the assumption that we are now living in a spiritual universe, that the law of our being is the Law of Mind in action, that there is an exact parallel between thought and things."

The Cosmos is In Order

As things are above, so are they below! The conditions in Heaven cast a shadow onto Earth and bring forth the conditions in our material realm. In a way, you are a shadow cast of God onto the surface of the earth, and since God is Mind and Spirit, so are you. Your physical body is nothing more than your shadow thinking it's a separate being. But just as the shadow cannot exist without the form on which the light shines, neither can you exist without the Light of God shining into the world. You and God are never separate; it is only your mind that creates this illusion.

In the parallel universe, the known and the unknown, the visible and invisible, exist side by side. Everything has an invisible, spiritual cause. But as long as Yahweh is King, enthroned in the heavens, the cosmos functions according to this parallel order. Everything runs according to the Laws God has laid down, and even God must obey them. In this way, God is the master conductor of the music of creation, and each of us is a different melodic line forming a great symphony of eternal harmony. There is nothing to fear and nothing but hope.

This order and sense of composition is why business and personal success are linked—parallel, again. You cannot be personally unhappy and be successful in business, because personal darkness will sabotage your ideas. We mirror each other's behavior and feelings thanks to those miraculous mirror neurons, so when you are unhappy, bitter or envious, people will not respond to your spirit. They will not serve your projects or help you reach your goals. And in business, nothing is accomplished alone. You will succeed based on self-knowledge, honesty and persistence, backed by the awareness of your thoughts as power sources.

Not Anxious, Just Aware

Anxiety is an epidemic among Americans, and it stems from the feeling that we are not in control of our lives. But there is no need for us to be anxious; we need only be aware and understand the nature of the parallel reality in which we dwell. Awareness brings the answers and the means of shaping and controlling our world to meet our ends—and bring about God's intent for our lives. When we are alert for the sacred signs and the opportunities to elevate our minds and cleanse our lives of want, we can create whatever we desire.

Whatever you see in the external, you may be assured has its parallel in mind.

Fillmore expresses our potential beautifully: "In mind, power is increased through exalted ideas. These show us the relation between the world without and the mind within, and we find that they are parallel. Whatever you see in the external, you may be assured has its parallel in mind. The same law is operating in the spiritual realm and the material realm under different masks of manifestation. The one thing to understand is that whatever we see without is controlled by something within. This law, once revealed to the mind, clears up the whole creation, and shows how God works. Man is the power of God in action."

Remember that God did not worry about the darkness. He simply said, "Let there be light." We have the power to do the same thing. Whatever we want is controlled by something within us. I'll share something extraordinary with you if you're ready. Are you ready?

〇 〇 〇

MAN IS THE POWER OF GOD IN ACTION.

〇 〇 〇

My goodness, that's immense! Amen! When we live according to the Laws and discipline our minds to exist in the reality of "I Am," we come back to God, like the prodigal son. Your purpose is to demonstrate the reality of this relationship, to demonstrate the truth that you are God in this world. Until people find themselves in this true and eternal nature, they will live in conflict and contradiction. If you know someone who seems to always be at war with himself and the better angels of his nature, it is because he is fighting the inner knowledge and his is a regent of God put on this earth to manifest his Divine nature. When we don't do our ordained jobs, we live in poverty. When we don't recognize what we are, we exist in spiritual poverty.

Cosmic Patterns

Parallels and patterns run throughout our station of existence. You can see them clustering in groups of seven: seven years for our bodies to completely change over all their cells, seven days for creation, seven chakras representing the seven "bodies" that coincide with our physical, mental and spiritual selves. This is worth knowing: every seven years, a different body matures—physical, emotional and so on. By the time we are 49 years old, our bodiless body, the pure Spirit that inhabits us all and turns our thoughts into things, matures. This is when we come into our own. This is when you should be able to see the future, even if you're not a prophet. We all have something of the prophet within us; we must mature into our perception to use it. This is why all of God's gifts are not given to us as children. We need to evolve.

> *Parallels and patterns run throughout our station of existence.*
>
> ☽ ☽ ☽

Money symbolizes this Divine nature. Money is the power to effect change in the physical world, because nothing in this material realm happens without money. Money is energy to move people; it is not just paper. The parallel nature of money is spiritual wealth: the ability to project your thoughts without hesitation or negativity into the ether and to *command* the universe to bring forth what you have already acquired in your mind. When you attain the power and discipline to do this, you will become rich. You will attract money without even trying, flowing to you from all directions. Money symbolizes your limitless flow of power and potential, because it is the freedom to pursue all paths and possibilities.

As Eric Butterworth writes, "As one man said, 'Since I became aware that I am an individualized expression of the infinite flow of substance, I feel prosperous at all times. And the most amazing thing is the way money flows to me from all directions. I simply can't keep it away from me.'" There was a man who had no pockets in his garments, because he believed that the world was his pocket. And this belief became self-fulfilling as the world gave the man everything that he needed in appropriate measure, and he knew no want but knew peace and joy. The world is your pocket if you can perceive and know it. Again, a parallel.

17

— THE LAW OF VIBRATION —

9 9 9

Know that from the vibration of the Word, we obtain spiritual wisdom and meditation. Through it, we speak the Unspoken. He is the fruit-bearing Tree, luxuriantly green with abundant shade. The rubies, jewels and emeralds are in the Guru's Treasury.

—*Sri Guru Granth Sahib*

Everything is relative—our position in the sky, our station in life, our relationship to the Almighty. And since everything in creation has a characteristic vibration frequency, it follows that all vibration is relative. The Law of Vibration says that you must learn to recognize the vibration of every being, object and spiritual state so you will know what is in harmony with your intentions and goals and what you should shun as being counter to God's intent. Our goal is to become vibration-literate.

Charles Fillmore expresses the reality of vibration quite eloquently: "Every idea originating in Divine Mind is expressed in the mind of man. Through the thought of man the Divine Mind idea is brought to the outer plane of consciousness. Through movement on what is termed the conscious, or most outer, plane of action, the thought takes expression as the spoken word. There is in the formed conscious man, or body, a point of concentration for this word. Through this point the word is expressed in invisible vibrations."

Those who can read and comprehend vibration can tell the difference between vibrations that indicate bliss or vanity; those who are blind to the subtle changes in vibrational frequency cannot do this. All words and thoughts are expressed in invisible vibration, so even when a person is not speaking and thinks you cannot read his intentions, if you can elevate your perceptions to a Divine pitch you can still assess his vibration and discover what kind of man he is. In this way, we can master the relationships that define so much of who we are.

Create Your Own Picture

Holmes in his writing makes an excellent analogy of the importance of vibration. When a person appears on television, the image and sound create vibrations which in turn become electromagnetic waves, vibrations that travel thousands of miles to be regenerated into comprehensible vocal sounds by another machine. But the heart of the process is vibration controlled by laws. The same type of process works for each of us as we try to walk the fine line between our physical and spiritual selves: we vibrate at a pitch unique to us and that vibration travels through the spiritual ether to regenerate in places unknown to us and affect things, people and outcomes there.

We all create our own pictures by our vibrations, and the effect of those pictures, under the absolute influence of the Laws of Being, determines much of who and what we become and how the world reacts to us. When we bring our consciousness up to the level of spiritual vibration, transcending the flesh and blood concerns of the world we see, we affirm our unity with divine substance. We undergo an organic regeneration much like that TV signal is regenerated in the minds of the people who see it. But in this case, we feel and absorb the vibrations of the Holy Spirit in our bodies and souls, the Spirit of God that inhabits and moves us.

Revelations 2:17 tells us, "He who has an ear, let him hear what the Spirit says to the churches. To him who overcomes, to him I will give some of the hidden manna, and I will give him a white stone, and a new name written on the stone which no one knows but he who receives it." When you can learn to raise your perception and always be aware of the vibrations of every creature and thing in the universe, you will hear Spirit loud and clear and be one of those who reap the rewards.

The Vibrating Mind

What causes vibration? The same force that causes everything else: Mind. Your mind, the state and condition of your thoughts, issues forth from your consciousness as a specific vibrational frequency, and others can sense it, even if they do not understand what it is. Have you ever met someone and taken an instant dislike to them for reasons you cannot understand? That's your mind sensing a vibration that is deeply in conflict with your own. You cannot have a relationship with that person until one of you changes his or her vibration.

Here's the key about vibration: everything we want and need vibrates with its own frequency

Here's the key about vibration: everything we want and need vibrates with its own frequency. But vibratory frequencies that are in conflict repel each other or cancel each other out; this a basic law of acoustics. This is how white noise machines work when you use them to block noise outside your bedroom so you can sleep at night: they issue sonic frequencies that cancel out the most common frequencies of things like traffic, construction noise and barking dogs. Well, if everything you want and need has its own vibration, what do you think you must do to manifest those things in your experience? Right—you must tune your personal vibration to the things you want.

Why do you think some spiritual gurus can bend metal with their minds, and others can touch a sick person and heal them instantly?

> ### *Whatever you vibrate at, that is what you will receive.*
>
> ### ා ා ා

It's not God working through them; it's them tuning their vibrations perfectly to complement and reinforce the vibration of whatever they are trying to achieve. If you want to change your world, change your vibration. Vibratory frequencies that are in harmony reinforce and strengthen each other, bringing them closer together. So when your mind is vibrating at a pitch that matches the pitch of good fortune, kindness to someone in need, or positive outcomes, those are what will come your way. Your vibration will press them out of the invisible.

On the other hand, if your vibration is on a level of want, desperation, anger or failure, that is all that will answer your vibration. Whatever you vibrate at, that is what you will receive. You can change your world by changing your vibration, but to do that you must change your habitual thinking.

Through You, Not To You

Florence Scovel Shinn writes, "All that the kingdom affords is yours. Every righteous desire of the heart is promised you. There are three thousand promises in the Bible, but these gifts can come to us only if we can believe them possible, for everything comes through you—not to you. All life is vibration. Feel rich, and you attract riches. Feel successful and you become successful."

This takes us back to the vital energy—the élan vital—of thought and how our thoughts, conscious or unconscious, pull outcomes from the spiritual plane into our material existence. The fact is, everything comes *through* you, not *to* you. What does this mean? It means that you are conduit for Divine energy that is channeled by your mind. The state of your thoughts and emotions is *everything*. Divine energy works through you to regenerate experiences, people, things and outcomes out of pure vibration. Vibration is the coin of the realm in the spiritual plane, and it brings

> *It means that you are conduit for Divine energy that is channeled by your mind.*
>
> ☉ ☉ ☉

about what you have in your corporeal existence. So your state of mind is a self-fulfilling prophecy. How you think, how you feel, how you talk to yourself and how open you allow your mind to be to the spiritual nature of reality determines what you will receive in this life.

You attract like vibrations, so what you want you must BECOME. Wow! That means if I want peace, I must change my vibrations with my mind to become peace personified—I must radiate peace in my waking life in this world. If I want wealth, I must become wealth. I must visualize wealth in spiritual realization, then adjust my mind to tune my vibrations to the pitch of wealth. Thoughts of want, lack and need are banished! Gone! Unwelcome! Only then will I attract wealth to myself in multiple ways. Shinn expresses this beautifully:

"You can never do a thing you cannot see yourself doing, or fill a place you cannot see yourself filling - not visualizing, making a mental picture (this is a mental process and often brings wrong and limited results); it must be a spiritual realization, a feeling that you are already there; be in its vibration."

Base Your Plans on Truth

The Law of Vibration is why so many people who become success-ful on the surface by lying, cheating, corrupting and breaking man's laws end up broken and bereft in the end. You can't fool vibration. You can say what you like on the surface and many people will believe (especially if you're helping them get rich), but vibration is not fooled. Your vibration will attract that which is like you, always. If you harbor evil in your heart, evil will always come to you. Look at O.J. Simpson. He was acquitted of his wife's murder and given his freedom, and what did he do? He kept his same violent, destructive vibration and a few years later he wound up back on trial again. There is no escaping your vibration.

> *You can't fool vibration.*
>
> ☾ ☾ ☾

Therefore, plans not based on the truth of who you are will be doomed to failure. If your intentions are discordant with your vibrations, you will be like Sisyphus pushing the boulder uphill in Dante's Hell: never able to reach your goal. Ever hear an orchestra warming up? It's a cacophony of conflicting, warring sounds. It's terrible. But when the conductor taps his baton and everyone begins playing on the same vibratory plane, the result is pure harmonic magic. Discord is destructive; harmony is creative. You can be like an orchestra warming up or one playing Beethoven's Fifth. The choice, as always, is your own.

The other thing about the nature of vibration is this: every vibration seeks a match for its frequency. Much like electrons that are always seeking to pair up (which is one of the causes of cell damage in our bodies), spiritual vibrations do not want to exist alone; they seek a partner. So if you are thinking positive thoughts and casting your Divine intention for health and prosperity into the ether, some vibration will respond. You will attract a like vibration to you. The opposite is true also. All vibrations seek their mate, so be careful how you tune your mind! You can't be sure what you will attract, and you don't want to attract misfortune, disease or evil into your life. Good reason to govern your consciousness.

All vibrations seek their mate, so be careful how you tune your mind!

ᘁ ᘁ ᘁ

The Magic of Believing

There's a self-help cliché that goes, "What you believe you can achieve." It's a cliché because it's true. A feeling is always accompanied by a corresponding vibration, so when you believe you can do something—or when you believe you can't—you're always right. Your vibration makes it so. As Neville Goddard wrote, "The subjective mind vibrates according to the modifications it undergoes by the thought and feelings of the operator. The visible state created is the effect of the subjective vibrations. A feeling is always accompanied by a corresponding vibration, that is, a change in expression or sensation in the operator."

Thus prosperity is never a sign of strained vibrations. Prosperity doesn't come to those whose vibrations are in conflict with their goals. If you meet someone who is truly successful in wealth, health, relationships and spirit, you will always find a person whose mental, physical and spiritual vibrations are completely in harmony with what he or she has achieved. This is why for some people success seems contagious. They seem to go from strength to strength, attracting good people and opportunity in their wake. It's because their vibration is attracting good and plenty to them.

Thus prosperity is never a sign of strained vibrations.

◯ ◯ ◯

In the same way, strain in vibration repels prosperity. Think of the twelve spies of the Promised Land. In this scenario, one day of pleasure equals 1 year of prosperity. The more pleasure and hope the spies found, the more God would yield up to them. But it didn't work that way. Ten of the twelve came back with reports of hardship and hunger—40 days worth. God rewarded them with 40 years wandering in the desert. That was an outcome they made themselves, because the Laws are absolute.

The Nature of Physical Energy

Think about what all this means for your life's goals: when you're working and straining to make prosperity happen, all that physical labor is just a vehicle for expressing mental energy. Physical power is the crudest form of energy, with a slow vibration. It is not mind; it is merely the reflection, the outcome, of the work of the mind. Mental energy is the highest form of energy and the fastest vibration, with emotional energy in the middle. As Catherine Ponder writes, "Once you learn how to release the highest form of energy and power into a situation, the lower, weaker forms of energy do not respond to you anymore. Physical energy is a slowed-down vibration that has limited power in the midst of accelerated mental and spiritual vibrations."

So to achieve what you wish, the body, the source of physical energy, must be in synch with the vibrations of the mind. Only when this occurs can you manifest health, wealth and wholeness. When the sanctuary that is your body is synchronized with powerful spoken and thought truth, there is a transformation. Your body becomes a kind of vibrational broadcast antenna that radiates positive vibrations and attracts wellness and wealth. This is why it is so important to go to church: every service reminds us of where our minds and bodies need to be. Every service is a healing!

Your mental vibration makes decrees that power through the psycho-reactive stuff of the Divine universe and attract eventual material outcomes into your life. So what are your vibrations decreeing? The truth of this is fundamental to the operation of the universe; vibration is how God conducts His business of ordering the cosmos. When you speak or think, you send out vibrations with the power of life or death into reality, vibrations with the power to reach out and guide events. Guard and discipline your mind!

Guard and discipline your mind!

Ↄ Ↄ Ↄ

Find Your Sanctuary

The power of vibration means that merely living as a conscious being is a vast responsibility. Your thoughts and words can topple kingdoms, heal the sick or change destinies. But in this noisy, distracting world, how can we shape and mold our vibrations? I have found that the best way is to find a time and place to retreat into the sanctuary of your mind, into prayer or meditation.

Go into that silent place in your spirit and just be there. Do this in a physical location where you will not be disturbed. Be very still and let your mind feel the singing of your spirit and the Divine music of the universe that resonates within you. Your body and mind are in tune and ready to radiate the vibration of health and happiness throughout the world, to all you come into contact with. Healing and harmony flow through you and from there, into the experience of others. You feel limitless joy and possibility. This is what you should do daily; it is a practice like any other. Over time, you will find the skill to tune your vibration to the perfect pitch.

You feel limitless joy and possibility.

೧ ೧ ೧

As you find the center of your natural Godly vibration, you will understand the nature of Being and Becoming. All life is in motion, but at the center is something eternal and unmoving, like the eye of a storm. All movement and vibration comes from this immobile heart. This is the Mind and Spirit of God. Expressed through you, they find motion and completion.

Truth Moves Mountains

As I said earlier, it is impossible to lie and achieve what you desire. You cannot think one way and act another and get a desired outcome. You will always be in conflict, like adjacent notes on a keyboard played together. Harmony becomes dissonance and the result is chaos and pain.

Truth moves mountains when our thoughts and actions are both in harmony with our innate vibrations. But discord cancels out positive vibrations and ruins our ability to radiate good and make good happen. We attract what we become, so if you want to attract a certain result in your life, you must first become that result in your mind! Become the wealth! Become the health! Become the rewarding relationships and the good fortune! You must visualize and fully accept a state in your mind where those are your reality, knowing that physical reality is nothing more than a *delayed reflection* of mental reality.

The first step: love everyone. Love is the ultimate power of God and the energy source by which everything else good is created in your experience. When you radiate vibrations of love, you put in motion mighty energies that bring the products of that love to you greatly multiplied. You will experience returned love, respect, honor, kindness, compassion, opportunity and great wisdom when love is the ground state of your vibration.

Charles Fillmore wrote, "Man is the power of God in action. The mind and the body of man have power to transform energy from one plane of consciousness to another. This is the power and dominion implanted in man from the beginning. It is man's control over his thoughts and feelings." Our true nature is linked to God, a role of great responsibility and gravity. We are here to express and impress God's intention on this world, to help it evolve to a higher state over time through our own vibratory wisdom. We do this through exalted thought. The power of the mind increases when exalted ideas flow through it— ideas about limitless possibility, human divinity, creating peace, endless kindness to those in need, boundless love. Those are the highest conditions to which we can aspire, because they reflect the limitless nature of the Mind from which we sprang.

We build our world thought by thought. Thoughts cast a stone into the pool of the invisible mental world, creating vibrations that radiate into eternity. Those vibrations bring about consequences, many of which we will never know of, and some of those consequences affect us and alter our vibrations. In this way, rage breeds rage, need breeds need and love breeds love. Most of all, vibrations move other minds. They can inspire, terrify, heal, confuse, soothe and protect. They are the way we reach out to others and shape their actions. The sophisticated thinker with a strong, positive mind, has the vibration to change the world for the better—in his and God's image.

18

— THE LAW OF OPULENCE —

ᘎ ᘎ ᘎ

Many speak the truth *when they say that they despise riches, but they mean the riches possessed by others.*

—Charles Caleb Colton

Opulence is your natural state of being. You are meant to be rich according to your kind and your values. For some, wealth will mean multiple homes or mansions around the world, while for others, it will mean having financial security with enough time to spend with family and friends while making a difference in the community. Your definition of wealth is automatically correct for you.

But it is important to remember that wealth is naturally yours—it flows to you in rivers of gold from Spirit, and all you do when you do not live immersed in the Laws of Being and the creative Mind is block it! Understand that wealth and opulence are always knocking at the door, trying to get through to you, and if you don't have them, you are doing something to prevent them from manifesting in your experience. There is no lack in your consciousness; you can imagine all the prosperity in the world. But when you focus on *getting* the blessing, you are focused on want. Want generates want. Remember, you will get what you become. To realize wealth, you must *become* your blessing. You already are your blessing! You have but to see it.

Deuteronomy 1:11 says, "May the Lord, the God of your fathers, increase you a thousand times and bless you as he has promised!" God has promised each of us an increase of a thousandfold. All we have to do is claim it. That so many do not, points to the need for greater spiritual education.

Opulence is Your Birthright

Opulence is your natural state. No one, not the hungriest villager in Africa, was meant to live in want. As long as your idea of prosperity does not hurt you or anyone else, and as long as it respects the earth that God gave us, you are entitled to have your dreams come into manifestation. Entitled! Good is flowing to you from all directions, if you can tune your vision and vibration to perceive and grasp it.

Opulence is your natural state.

೦ ೦ ೦

What is opulence? The dictionary defines it as, "Wealth as evidenced by sumptuous living." But what is sumptuous living? It is living richly in the spirit, not necessarily in material possessions. There are retired couples who own their home, have passions and hobbies and many friends and wonderful, extended families who do not inhabit mansions but are rich, and people who live in huge homes with boats and private jets who are impoverished. It all depends on how rich your conscious-ness is and how in tune your vibration is with who and what you are. Opulence means it all works—your thought, your action, your spirit, your meditation, your connection with God and Man—to bring you everything you want, your personal vision of wealth. That is your birthright: to have your dreams come true.

This represents the ultimate responsibility. There truly is no one else to blame or thank for your prosperity or ill fortune. It's all you. Willis H. Kinear writes, "The ability to control your experiences and have them result in happiness, prosperity, and success lies in your own mind and the way you use it. This means you control your own experience— you are really in charge of your affairs and the way they are to develop. Let us sum it up this way: My thought is in control of my experience and I can direct my thinking." Your thoughts determine what you become and how you live, and you are in control of your thinking. Thought is a habit. You have all the power and choice.

Substance = Supply

One of the criticisms leveled at this newly evolving spiritual reality is that it is materialistic and shallow, focusing only on the gaining of wealth instead of good works. Critics call this "the prosperity gospel," as though there is something evil about prosperity, or as though some- one living in poverty has much freedom to do good works. This is evil, separating substance from supply, man from God.

Life must be lived and it must be lived simultaneously in this world and the next, and if you are focused on pure survival, you will not be free to grow in spirit or help your fellow man. Who is it that works most of the good in this world, from funding AIDS prevention in Africa to promoting literacy? The rich! They have the means and more importantly, they have the freedom of mind and the time. They are not spending all their days trying to keep from losing their house. Prosperity gospel? Yes, amen! Prosperity cures the world's ills, and we should continue to seek it.

The false separation of this materialistic thinking also leads some people to see God as an outside force, a bearded judge on a throne. But we know that God is within us, seeking to reveal Himself in us and AS us. This is why the Pharisees and Sagisees, the warring gangs of Jesus' time, did not understand what He preached. They saw God and man as separate, and this is mistaken. Jesus called them "a generation of vipers and scorpions." Well, did you know that with some breeds of scorpion, when the baby is born it eats its way out of its mother, killing her, and then kills its father? That symbolic killing of the Father is what such separatist thinking does.

Wherever God is, you are.

ɔ ɔ ɔ

Wherever God is, you are. There is no separation. God and man are one. Money and good works are one. Prosperity is the power of change. For what can happen in our world without it? False prophets, they are who preach the virtues of poverty. Let them experience poverty and then speak of its virtues!

Opulence is Inevitable

So there is nothing to be ashamed of in working to develop your consciousness to become the wealth that you want to manifest in your physical experience. In fact, opulence is the unavoidable consequence of being in your right mind, stating your "I Am" and tuning your consciousness to the creative energy of the invisible. If you do this, opulence will come to you. Period. Once you have an irresistible *subjective* image of what you want in your mind and once that image is as real to you as this book you're reading, the *objective* thing will come to you. It is a Divine necessity.

It is part of your nature and increases with your goodness. This is the meaning behind karma and the phrase "what goes around comes around." The more good deeds you work, the greater your mind becomes in coordination with the Divine Mind, and the more good comes to you. Giving becomes a wealth strategy, which is why so many wealthy people do it!

Charles Fillmore wrote, "There is an invisible thought-stuff on which the mind acts, making things through the operation of a law not yet fully understood by man. Every thought moves upon this invisible substance in increasing or diminishing degree." Fillmore understood that the nature of reality—what we see as real in our material existence—is actually produced by the invisible stuff of the psyche. So whatever ideals we hold in our minds become real for us. Think on something long enough and it comes to pass. Turn your attention to a thing and it comes into your awareness. When your thought is Divine and orders creation to occur, transformation results.

Turn your attention to a thing and it comes into your awareness.

It is the Father's pleasure for you to have opulence. This is hard for many to accept. So often we associate wealth with corruption, as if having a high income can fundamentally alter a person's character. No, much as adversity does, wealth does not shape character; it reveals it. Still, we persist in this idea of wealth as corrupt and poverty as virtuous. Therefore, any limitation on our ability to achieve opulence comes from our sense of guilt or unworthiness. But this is a cultural limitation; it has no validity in the Mind of God. Still, it limits many people. Light is the oldest substance in the universe, yet it must conform to the aperture in which it is projected. Your light may be potentially limitless, but if you place your consciousness in a box you will not achieve what would otherwise be inevitable.

Opulence is your inheritance from Jesus, but you must claim it in order to experience it. Part of my goal in revealing the Laws of Being and of Becoming is to empower you to see your role in the universe with new eyes. As Malinda Cramer writes, "To be rich in Being is to be rich in mentality and is to be rich visibly. Then let us lay hold of the riches of Being, locate our wealth, so that we can prove our opulence. Let us sow freely, give forth full measure and we shall reap bountifully and receive abundantly."

Money Is Not the Point

Here's where the difficult lies: you should not focus on making money. Is this a contradiction? No. Let me explain. Your wealth is of your consciousness, so your aim should be to become rich in consciousness and thought, to be rich in your oneness with God's purpose and system, and let the chips fall where they may. You cannot go wrong when you take this route, because you become the wealth in your mind that will eventually come to you in your material experience. But when you "try to make money," you are acknowledging in your mind that you do not have it, and the universe will respond to that want. Be what you want to see! As Solomon said in Proverbs 4:7, "With all thy getting, get understanding." Focus on your mind and money will come.

Focus on your mind and money will come.

૭ ૭ ૭

Eric Butterworth wrote that to focus on getting money is a sure way to pull yourself out of the flow of universal substance. Suddenly your attention is not on mind but on baser material things. You are working with the sweat of your brow and not the limitless energies of your mind. You are embracing limitation. Opulence is about understanding how wealth flows: from the single thought to the habitual thought to the "I Am" beingness to the invisible force to the eventual material reality. The word *affluence* actually means "to flow forth."

Spiritual opulence is a fundamental law of the cosmos. To achieve it, you must raise your vibration to the level of consciousness that is equal to the thing you envision in your mind. The greater your desired achievement, the purer your Divine consciousness, untainted by any human doubt or fear, must be. A man with the vision of having his home paid off will need a lower level of vibration than a man whose vision is for the funds to build health clinics for every poor village in South America. But as you learn and grow, you will gain the proficiency and elevating your consciousness to higher and higher levels.

> *Spiritual opulence is a fundamental law of the cosmos.*

Why Not Be Wealthy?

In his play *No Exit,* famously depressive existentialist writer and philosopher Jean-Paul Sartre wrote, "Hell is other people." I agree, partially. I actually think Hell is negative people, because their destructive vibration fans out like a plume of pollution in ground water and poisons those of us who are near them. This is why it is so important to control with whom you associate. Negative people warp your vibrations and can affect the people who come into your life and the opportunities you find.

The funny (or sad) thing is, it is just as easy to think from a place of opulence as it is to be negative and self-defeating, so why not do so? Why not lift your thoughts and your intentions to creating wealth and good for yourself and others, just in case it works? I think those who cannot are creating their own private Hell.

Another good piece of advice is, never go to sleep in wrath. You've no doubt heard this admonishment in relation to arguments between couples as, "Never go to bed angry." Good advice, but it even applies if you're single. If you sleep in anger, your mind continues to work—continues planting and harvesting a new reality. This will be what you will have tuned into the next day; anger and rage in your sleep could send you down a path to sorrow or unhappy chance. Remember, as Florence Scovel Shinn wrote, "Every man has within himself a gold nugget; it is his consciousness of gold, of opulence, which brings riches into his life. In making his demands, man begins at his journey's end, that is, he declares he has already received. 'Before ye call I shall answer.' Continually affirming establishes the belief in the subconscious."

Another good piece of advice is, never go to sleep in wrath.

You Are Created for Opulence

Prosperity is your natural state; allowing yourself to be impoverished is actually defying the intent of God. You were made to enjoy abundance as the child of a rich father—which you are. Jesus said, "I come that you may have life and have it more abundantly." He didn't say, "I come that you can be poor and scuffle in this life only to die and go into the afterlife angry." Plenty is your birthright.

Plenty is your birthright.

ᓂ ᓂ ᓂ

And it doesn't depend on where you come from, where you went to school or where you live. Look at rap stars who are millionaires; do you think they went to Ivy League schools? Look at Oprah, who came from an abusive home. These people had passion and belief and indomitable thought and they *forced* their visions to become reality. They *refused* to take no for an answer from the universe. Moses learned about opulence while he was in the court of Pharaoh, but his journey did not end there. He later discovered mystical and practical opulence and their relationship, leading his people into a land of milk and honey. But the people did not understand how their negative energies would divert Moses' great mind; for every day they complained, they were sentenced to a year wandering in the wilderness before they finally reached Canaan. If they had remained faithful and shared Moses' vision, they would have reached it sooner.

The Bible echoes this in Job 36:11, which reads, "If they hear and serve Him, they will end their days in prosperity and their years in pleasures." Being God in mind brings us to our destined wealth much sooner than toil. And opulence is a necessity for your inner and outer success. You should not worship in poor surroundings; this is why Exodus gave the Hebrews such specific instructions for the tabernacle. Your surroundings shape your mind, such as a bedroom done in relaxed colors and fabrics, with incense and music, frees you to be more at peace. So being in opulent surroundings makes your consciousness richer still. It becomes easier to dwell on positive visions and great goals. If your sanctuary is a poor shack with no heat, it is very hard to avoid thoughts of want and lack.

In the end God guides you into opulence by faith. There is no fear, no want, no need that you are not equal to. When you dream greatly, you can have perfect health, truth, joy and love. God is magnified when you are prosperous. So condition your mind for opulence. Actively shed those ideas about the holiness of poverty. Realize that wealth is what you make of it and if your mind is right, your hands will overflow with gold yet your heart will remain golden for others. Luke 12:31 reads, "But seek His kingdom, and these things will be added to you." Know that you are a rich and healthy child of God and your dreams cannot help but come true.

19

— THE LAW OF DEMAND —

○ ○ ○

Power concedes nothing without a demand. It never did and it
never will.

—*Frederick Douglass*

The Law of Demand states that the demand you place into the
universe will come back to you. So watch what you live by, because
there are many ways to place a demand. The most obvious way is by
what you say, and that is the reason it is so vital to learn to command
your tongue. Watch your habit of saying negative things, doubting your
own abilities or predicting bad outcomes. Few demands resonate into
the ether and produce direct effects like spoken thought.

But speech is not the only interface with cosmic computer that is
reality. Thought is your next most powerful method of issuing demands
and potentially the most dangerous, because few of us possess the
mental discipline to govern our minds and avoid the stray negative or
self-defeating thought. One single poisonous thought can sabotage
everything you are trying to do! A great business startup might be going

along smoothly until you have a bad week where several customers don't pay you on time. Briefly, you allow your mind to dwell on your anger and frustration before catching yourself and returning to positive thoughts. Too late: your negative thoughts cast a demand into the waters of the cosmos and will bring some unfortunate consequence. It may not wreck your business, but it will be enough to ruin your day. So we must be especially vigilant about the demands our thoughts project.

But your emotions and actions also issue demands, as do the associations you maintain. It is vital that you associate with people who reflect the success and wealth you wish to become, because hanging with people who harbor negative attitudes, blame others or think only of themselves will affect the tenor of your congress with the unseen. Think of your interaction with the immaterial stuff of fulfilled dreams as a constant stream of water that nourishes your future. When your demand is tainted by word or deed, that water becomes polluted. Dreams can't grow to their healthy fullness; sick results come to you.

Free Yourself

You owe no one an explanation for this! You are the only one in charge of your ship; you don't even owe an explanation to God. He has created the conditions under which you can survive or struggle and while He wants you to thrive, He will not interfere if you choose to struggle. So whatever you need to do to improve your mind, thoughts and the demands you project into the world, you do, no excuses. Free yourself from the demands of others. As long as you do not hurt or rob others of their opportunity, you have nothing to explain.

Free yourself from the demands of others.

○ ○ ○

This proactive stance allows you to be the cause of the things that come into your life, not the effect. You can be the spark, not the flame, no longer being reactionary to what occurs. This is HUGE. We live in today's scientific world under the seeming sentence that life has no meaning or purpose and that all that occurs is the result of random chance. That actually may be the case for people who do not exercise any control over their lives and do not express their "I Am" to the universe in any way. However, when you do project your demand and will into reality, you can predict what will happen to a great degree. Not all things, because you are as a rock surrounded by the ocean, buffeted by many forces—stray thoughts, emotions, the intentions of others, your associations—but many things. You gain greater control over your destiny!

You can be the spark, not the flame,

As Holmes writes, "No longer am I acted upon by my world. I now am *cause* to my world. I act in mind, and my world reacts in matter in direct response to my demand. I am cause, not effect. I am Spirit releasing Itself into form under freedom."

So the demand you place determines the result you will see. This is the essence of "I Am." Coming into your "I Am" state is demanding of the invisible material of dreams that it brings something corporeal into your experience. It is becoming God. As Holmes describes it, whenever we create an idea, we make a demand on the Mind of God that is incarnated in us. With that demand, supply can come into being. That is the natural law upon which the universe created and continues to create itself. God created the Laws of Being and Becoming to set current and future creation in motion, handling the clockwork and evolution of all that it so He could focus His attention and intention on the development of Spirit.

The Nature of the Future

As you may have appreciated by now, the act of using thought and word to demand service of God's cosmic economy is, in part, also playing with time. Concepts like past and future break down when we find that we can command the future from the present. That is reaching into the timestream to command the future to take shape according to our will. That is truly Divine.

However, we have limits. The future does not unfold in accordance with anyone's desires, but

Want in your mind brings want in your reality.

☾ ☾ ☾

according to natural Laws. The Laws are impersonal, so the future must also be. You can powerfully desire to have wealth and buy your own house, but despite this strong desire, if your state of mind is needy and weak and negative and want-based, you will never receive that result. Want in your mind brings want in your reality. The Laws have no choice but to bring it to you, as the law of gravity has no choice but to pull a ball back to earth.

So this brings up another truth about demand: do not demand of others. Vernon Howard writes, "It is a great mistake to try to please people who demand to be pleased. Satisfy one demand and two more demands will arise. Neurotic needs are never satisfied. A demanding mind is like a hammer that sees everything as a nail. Remember that and stay out of the way. You owe nothing to demanding people." When you make demands, you are acknowledging that you are not the result you desire;

you need the help of another to get that result. That is want-based thinking and want will be your reward! You cannot force things to happen; you must become the victory or the goal and let it come to you in its own time. This is what the law of attraction is all about: being the goal and then allowing it to find you. And find you it always will.

The Root of All Creation

Consciousness is the substance of all things seen and unseen. This defies the human laws of supply and demand, which insist that a man must look outside himself to satisfy his needs. But that is falsehood; you cannot find anything of value outside yourself, because consciousness is the currency that moves every economic wheel in existence. When you look outside for support and wealth, you are again acknowledging that you are not the solution, you are not that result that you seek. That, as we have seen, is a trap that materialists constantly fall into. If the answer to what you seek does not lie within your mind, then you are seeking the wrong thing!

Consciousness is the substance of all things seen and unseen.

Nothing works unless you keep it in circulation. This is a mystical secret. Money only has power when it is circulating and working as energy to move bodies and minds. Otherwise it is just paper. Think of yourself as a tree in a river of water. By simply being in that river, you change its course. You affect the movement, the current, the eddies and whirlpools of the stream. By being in this psycho-active reality, you affect its unseen swirls and currents. Mind is always circulating; outcomes are always coming into manifestation in your life, 24 hours a day.

You don't always perceive them, but they are there. How you circulate your thoughts and make your demands decides what you will manifest. How are you circulating?

The beauty of all this is that because of the nature of consciousness as Source of all, we are freed from Adam Smith economics, want and supply and demand. Once we come into God Consciousness, we no longer have to worry about economic gyrations and talk of recession. There is never a recession in the spiritual economy. There is as much plenty as your mind allows to appear in your awareness. No matter what you desire, God's grace can meet the demand. The raw material of dreams is without limit.

Don't Be Timid

So the saying is true, "Fortune favors the brave." You cannot sit back, as many people I see do, and wait for God to bring you something you want. It doesn't work that way. I have seen many passive people comfort themselves that if they just pray and wait and suffer eventually God will reward them. This is nonsense. God rewards will and intention and demands made in the spirit of "I Am." He does not reward passivity. One of the best known sayings in Christianity is, "The Lord helps those who help themselves." Now you know what it really means.

Life will always bring you what you ask for and expect according to the nature of your demands. So there's no point in being timid; demand what you want! Either you know and accept your value as a Divine being, or you deny it. Which is it? You must actively demand, through faith, that the spiritual realm release the latent energy of creation and change and channel it toward you. That energy is not yours by right, any more than it is anyone else's. But when you pay for it with your attention and intention, you reap the supply. It's like turning on a faucet in a public park: the water belongs to everyone in theory, but because you started the slow, you get to take as much as you need.

However, the Law of Demand requires "right thinking." You must become as disciplined as a monk in controlling your mind at all times, else you shall inadvertently demand enemies and illness in your life. Right thinking means maintaining a tightly commanded mental state of positive thinking, expectation of good, awareness that you *are* the result you seek, and belief in your eventual, destined receipt of the good in your material life. This is what Vernon Howard calls "being awake." Unawakened people bring dangerous relationships and poor outcomes upon themselves.

Don't Be Dependent

Another thing that I see all too often is people abdicating their responsibility for their own lives to others. They say, "So-and-so will take care of me." This is a fatalism almost as hazardous as relying on God to be your magic genie, fulfilling your wishes. Dependency is a guaranteed way to sabotage your coming prosperity! Dependency creates unhealthy demands because it teaches you to internalize that you are helpless and unworthy of great results. It negates your oneness with God and casts you into separation. Most of all, dependency distracts you from the inner search that leads to greater will, self-awareness and right thought.

Dependency is a guaranteed way to sabotage your coming prosperity!

But self-dependency removes the possible harm from your mind. This is the attitude you must cultivate: you are responsible for every outcome in your life. There is nothing that comes to you that is not a reflection of who you are and what you have allowed your energy to do. There is a subtle yet astonishing reason for this, expressed by the brilliant Joel Goldsmith. He reasons that man is called to be perfect, because man is the expression of God pressed out into the material world, and since God is perfect, man must strive to be as well.

He writes, "Is not God greater than we are? Is not the love of God greater than any love that we can express? Are not the wisdom and the justice of God greater than the wisdom and justice of man? To ascribe evil in any form to God is to make God lower than man, for of man it is demanded, 'Be ye therefore perfect, even as your Father which is in heaven is perfect,'" We have perfection within us, each of us, down to the most pathetic homeless person or the most debased drug addict. All of us are God enfleshed, and all of us bear the seeds of perfection. We have a duty and obligation to express that potential and grow into our status as God.

Know You Are Free!

We can no longer afford to be ignorant of these principles that make us free. We live in an age when materialism runs rampant and when happiness has been replaced by the need to consume. We mistake our hunger for material goods with the satisfaction that comes with becoming who we know we were destined to become. One is transitory; the other is eternal. You must see past the façade of the material world and understand that wealth for its own sake is empty. Wealth in the service of God's intent is miraculous.

Wealth in the service of God's intent is miraculous.

Ↄ ↄ Ↄ

It is the duty of each of us to be free in spirit, to inhabit the invisible world where Spirit reigns, not to be body bound. Our bodies limit us; they get sick, grow old and die. They impose upon us at inopportune times and seem to enslave us, but only if we let them. Only if we dwell in the body are we limited. Instead, the mind and spirit must be the vehicles of our evolution, with our bodies the fine instruments at the mind's command. Truth is everything; the truth about what you are, not just who you are, will set you free.

Your false self is harmful to your dreams. It demands certain behavior from others and when it doesn't receive that behavior, becomes enraged. You cannot control the physical realm of reality; you cannot control what other bodies do. Your control and command lives in the mental and spiritual realms alone. There can you mold and shape events and create your future. Life demands that you make decisions based on this reality. "Choose ye this day," says Scripture. Thought and intention must circulate to be effective—to circulate, you must make demands. Direct the cosmos to bring you what you have already become and do it often. Work the Divine system and keep the wheels turning! Stillness is a sign of death; life is about demands and the result of those demands. Make many decisions every day, take responsibility for them, and expect them to bring you good.

This belief in good outcomes is crucial. That which you believe will appear through the creative process of the invisible substrate of existence that ties Mind to Matter. The more you repeat the reality of what you will into being, the more you believe and know that it is coming to your material experience, the quicker and more completely it will manifest. Demand everything and receive everything! There is no limit!

You are free. Free of the limitations of supply and demand. When you create demand, a void appears that supply must fill. That void, that hunger, is the Divine speaking within us. When Jesus transmuted the water into wine to serve the wedding guests, he did not wave his hand and change the matter. That's impossible. He declared the void to exist and the supply of wine came into being as if the water had never been. That is the power of understanding—and making—demands. As we read in Mark 11:24, Therefore I say unto you, what things soever ye desire, when ye pray, believe that ye receive them, and ye shall have them."

20

— THE LAW OF RIGHT ACTION —

꧆ ꧆ ꧆

You can either take action, or you can hang back and hope for a miracle. Miracles are great, but they are so unpredictable.

—Peter Drucker

Finally, we come to the Law of Right Action. Right action always bears fruit in this world, as Matthew says in the Bible: "You will know them by their fruits. Grapes are not gathered from thorn bushes nor figs from thistles, are they?" The Law of Right Action is that right thinking always leads to right action, and right action to the outcomes that dwell in your deepest desires. There are no obstacles that can stand in the way of this reality.

All enlightened people operate in the Christ-mind. Eric Butterworth writes, "Through the Christ-Mind you are unified in thought, purpose, and understanding, and inspired to right action for the security and freedom of all mankind." Christ, as seen by many philosophers such as Howard Thurman (and myself) was no different than any other man. He did not come to reveal Himself to us, but to reveal us to ourselves. He came to show Man how he could live in and with the attitude of Christ, always dwelling in Right Mind, always with the channel between belief and actuality open and thrumming with energy and possibility. We can live this way if we train our minds. We become what we understand, and in that understanding lies our becoming God. That is our natural destiny. The Laws exist in the end so that Man can become God, as God once became Man.

Wrong Thinking, Wrong Action

Of course, the opposite is also true. It must be according to natural law. Wrong thinking will bring wrong action as surely as night brings dawn. When we are not in cosmic consciousness, we are engaged in wrong thinking. Vernon Howard writes about this, "Our self-examination must reach the point where we are willing to let go of the pretence of having control over particular habits or life in general. We may do it timidly at first, but we finally let go because we now see it as right action and the only action possible. By seeing that we cannot do anything, doing becomes possible, but it is not our personal power. It is Cosmic Action."

We gain destiny by giving up the illusion of control.

๑ ๑ ๑

This is a paradox in which God exists eternally. By giving up the sense of physical control of life, we surrender our egos to the spiritual reality that we can bring our future into the present with cosmic consciousness. We gain destiny by giving up the illusion of control.

You must continually perform right action, action unified by mind and spirit. Your actions must serve a single destination, a single goal. You must learn to see the ebb and flow of things. Becoming one with